FREDERICK MANFRED

MIDWEST  REFLECTIONS

Memoirs and personal histories of the people of the Upper Midwest

Frederick Manfred

A Daughter Remembers

‹ · ›   ‹ · ›   ‹ · ›

Freya Manfred

Mary Jeine —
for now & forever

Freya Manfred

Minnesota Historical Society Press · St. Paul

MIDWEST REFLECTIONS
Memoirs and personal histories of the people of the Upper Midwest

Publication of this book was supported in part by the
Elmer L. and Eleanor J. Andersen Publications Endowment Fund.

Manufactured in the United States of America

10 9 8 7 6 5 4 3 2 1

International Standard Book Number
0-87351-371-1 (cloth)   0-87351-372-X (paper)

♾ The paper used in this publication meets the minimum requirements of the
American National Standard for Information Sciences—Permanence for Printed Library
Materials, ANSI Z39.48-1984.

Library of Congress Cataloging-in-Publication Data

Manfred, Freya.
    Frederick Manfred : a daughter remembers / Freya Manfred.
       p.   cm.—(Midwest reflections)
    ISBN 0-87351-371-1 (cloth : alk. paper).—ISBN 0-87351-372-X (pbk. : alk. paper)
       1. Manfred, Frederick Feikema, 1912–   . 2. Authors, American—20th
    century—Family relationships.   3. Authors, American—20th century—Biography
    4. Fathers and daughters—Middle West.   5. Western stories—Authorship.
    6. Manfred, Freya.
    I. Title.   II. Series.
    PS3525.A52233Z76   1999
    813'.54—dc21
    [b]   98-54633

Some of the material in this book appeared earlier in a different form in *The Lizard
Speaks: Essays on the Writings of Frederick Manfred*, edited by Nancy Owen Nelson
(Sioux Falls, S.D.: The Center for Western Studies, 1998).

All photographs are from the collection of the author.

Dedicated to
the artist in America

CONTENTS

When the murky night   in the mist-cold winter
Falls on the fields   then fare all men safely
Into their house and garden   to preserve their lives.
Even the wild beast   seeks its home
In the hollow tree   its den in the rocks.
But the orphan child weeps,   he has naked limbs,
Lacks house and garden.   His father, who could help him
Turn away winter cold   and a burning hunger,
His father lies deep and dark   under oak and earth,
Because he is beslain and beshut and bedone.

Wanderlust

Poem found embedded in Old Frisian laws
and translated from the Frisian

PREFACE

It was all marvelous. I don't regret a minute of it.
Even the pain and hunger, the almost broken head
and the broken heart, were sweet to have. It was life;
not death. And all moments of life are very precious.
Duke's Mixture

THIS IS THE STORY OF THE SIX WEEKS WHEN MY FATHER,
the author Frederick Manfred, lay dying of brain cancer. It
is also an examination of the heart and fortitude of the artistic soul, told against a background of personal memories
and private letters, interwoven with excerpts from some of
Dad's novels. Although I had not read many of his novels for
more than twenty-five years when I began this memoir, I
was pleased to discover that bits and pieces of them came to
mind as I wrote. These excerpts are intended to stand as historical and metaphysical markers along the way so that the
reader may stop and remember Dad's work or be introduced
to it for the first time.

My father was born on a farm near Doon, Iowa, on January 6, 1912, in the heart of the American Middle West, and
he chose to live and write in Minnesota for the rest of his
life. As his complex and brilliant intelligence faded in and
out during his final days, I felt the kingdom of his imagina-
tion, a place he named Siouxland, dying with him. Despite
having written thirty-three books, he spoke every day of
wanting to "do something *more* for the arts in America."
This memoir is my attempt to do something more.

This is not a biography. Nor did my father write an autobiography, though he kept a diary and made copies of his

letters. A more detailed revelation of his personal and literary life can be found in *The Selected Letters of Frederick Manfred, 1932–1954*, edited by Arthur R. Huseboe and Nancy Owen Nelson and published in 1988 by the University of Nebraska Press.

As an aid to readers, I include the following list of books by Frederick Manfred:

The Golden Bowl (1944)
Boy Almighty (1945)
This Is the Year (1947)
The Chokecherry Tree (1948)
The Primitive (1949)
The Brother (1950)
The Giant (1951)
Lord Grizzly (1954)
Morning Red (1956)
Riders of Judgment (1957)
Conquering Horse (1959)
Arrow of Love (1961; short stories)
Wanderlust (1962; revised version of *The Primitive*, *The Brother*, and *The Giant*, published in one volume)
Scarlet Plume (1964)
The Man Who Looked like the Prince of Wales (1965; reprinted in paperback as *The Secret Place*)
Winter Count: Poems, 1934–1965 (1966)
King of Spades (1966)
Apples of Paradise and Other Stories (1968)
Eden Prairie (1968)
Conversations with Frederick Manfred (1974; moderated by John R. Milton)
The Manly-Hearted Woman (1975)
Milk of Wolves (1976)
Green Earth (1977)
The Wind Blows Free: A Reminiscence (1979)
Sons of Adam (1980)

Dinkytown (1984; chapbook)
Winter Count II: The Poems of Frederick Manfred (1987)
Prime Fathers (1988; essays)
Flowers of Desire (1989)
No Fun on Sunday (1990)
Of Lizards and Angels: A Saga of Siouxland (1992)
Duke's Mixture (1994; essays)
Moon Calf (unpublished)
The Wrath of Love (unpublished)
Black Earth (unpublished)

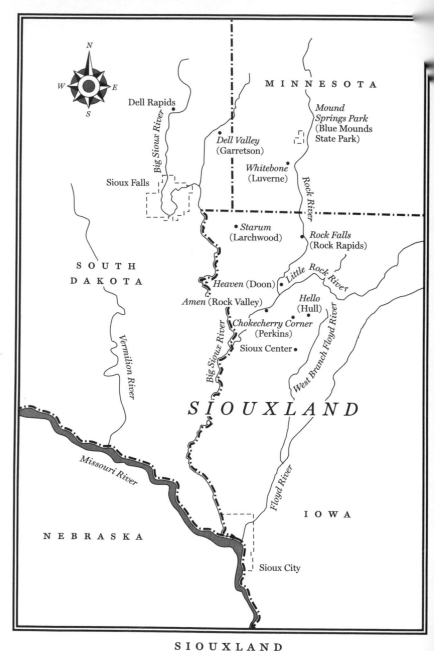

SIOUXLAND
Town names in italic are the ones Frederick Manfred used
in his novels set in Siouxland.

One

⟨ · ⟩   ⟨ · ⟩   ⟨ · ⟩

BURIAL

On the first night of the storm, Tollef lost his way and wandered over the desert's howling floor. In the doubly black night, solicitous of the animals, he had tried to walk the short way from the house to the barn. Two days later, when the wind let up, they found his body in a drouth-crevasse near the willows by the creek, smothered in a drift of flour-fine dust. Like a mountaineer on a glacier in a blizzard, he had not seen the yawning chasm ahead.

Dust drove through the cluster of bareheaded people that gathered in the churchyard. Dust filmed his coffin. Dust and the minister's word fell beside him in the grave.

The Golden Bowl

A PROCESSION OF CARS, LED BY A GRAY HEARSE bearing my father's coffin, left the George Boom Funeral Home in Sioux Falls, South Dakota, on September 10, 1994, crossed the Big Sioux River, and cut across the still-green bluffs into the rolling fields of northwest Iowa. As the motorcade slowed upon entering each small town, other drivers pulled to the side of the road and stopped, raising sheets of ditch dust that settled briefly on the crawling cortege and then blew off in the hot gusty winds.

The funeral procession continued under the deep blue sky for almost an hour, through cornfields and wheatfields, past farmyards and more towns, until it turned left and up-hill into the Hillside Cemetery just across the winding Rock River from Doon, Iowa, where my father was born almost eighty-three years before.

The hearse bounced to a stop beside a flapping blue canopy in the southwest corner. It was the highest part of the cemetery and still empty of gravestones. A group of mourners waiting beside the open grave watched with alert, sad, wondering faces as the plain pine coffin was lifted from the hearse by my father's three living brothers, Henry Feikema, Abben Feikema, and Floyd Feikema; his son, Frederick Manfred, Jr.; my husband, Tom Pope; and our fourteen-year-old sons, Ethan Rowan Pope and Nicholas Bly Pope.

The seven-foot-tall cornstalks north and west of the grave site thrashed wildly, fell silent, sighed, then thrashed again in the gusting wind. The mourners seated themselves on folding chairs while I laid armfuls of purple, yellow, and white wildflowers from Dad's hillside in Luverne on top of the coffin. A vase of red and white gladioli and lilies in front of the coffin blew over in a sudden gust of wind, and I set it back up, rearranging its ribbon, on which was written BROTHER.

> *September 28, 1981*
> *Dear Freya and Tom and boys,*
>   When I drove down this morning in the clear yellow air of early fall, I was reminded again, as I have been so many times on such mornings, of your wedding day. There were the same lazy slowly swirled mares' tails in the deep blue sky, the same slow cool breeze from the west, the same lovely shadows under the yellowing trees, the same ocher-and-green colors of the cornfield and alfalfa lands and pastures. I still savor the excitement of that wedding day, the "funs" we all had, the people who drove long distances, the drama around the "altar" rocks, the dinner afterwards, and so on. I also remember how, hanging over it in my head, in the back part of my head, was the thought that in a few days I'd fly to California to bury my 90 year old father. Talk about light and dark, heights and depths! Many people since that day, who were there, speak of it as the most dramatic and interesting wedding they ever saw. Same here.
> *Love, Dad*

The funeral began with a recording of original piano music composed and played by my sister, Marya Manfred. Then Fred welcomed everyone and, bowing, held Dad's Lakota peace pipe to the four directions and to heaven and earth.

The giant Minnesota poet, Bill Holm, rose with a reddened face, looked down over the Rock River, and, with a deep barrel-chested voice, sang "Shall We Gather at the River," followed by a reading from Walt Whitman, one of Dad's favorite poets. Another old friend of Dad's, the poet Robert Bly, his white hair rising and falling in the wind, read from Antonio Machado:

All things die and all things live forever;
but our task is to die,
to die making roads,
roads over the sea.

Benjamin Vander Kooi, a family friend and my father's trusted lawyer, read from Ecclesiastes. Uncle Henry, Dad's youngest brother, his voice soft with grief and love, read the keenly logical, manly-hearted poem Dad had requested, from "On the Nature of Things," by the Roman poet Lucretius:

Death
Is nothing to us, has no relevance
To our condition, seeing that the mind
Is mortal . . .
We may be assured that in our death
We have no cause for fear, we cannot be
Wretched in nonexistence. Death alone
Has immortality, and takes away
Our mortal life. It does not matter a bit
If we once lived before.

My husband, Tom, read "I Died for Beauty" by Emily Dickinson, Dad's favorite poet, "Sonnet V" by Edna St. Vincent Millay, and "Men's Tears," a poem I'd written for Tom's mother's funeral. Then another of Dad's old friends, Waring Jones, stood up and knocked on Dad's coffin and said, "Fred? You in there? I know you're not—you're in here," holding up one of Dad's best-selling novels, *Lord Grizzly*. He told a few stories about how Dad researched the novel by crawling around on all fours with one leg bound in a makeshift splint, eating grubs and ants to see how they would have tasted to the book's hero, old Hugh Glass.

When he opened his eyes once more, he saw it. His grave. Beside him, not a yard away, someone had dug a shallow grave for him, a grave some three feet deep and seven feet long.

Old gray eyes almost blinded with tears, with extreme pain, green bottleflies buzzing all around, he stared at it.

His grave.

He shook his head; blinked.

His grave.

So that was it. He was done for. His time was up.

His grave. He lay on his right side looking at it, bewildered in a wilderness.

"Ae, I see it now, lads. It's this old coon's turn at last."
Lord Grizzly

The poet John Calvin Rezmerski read from the last pages of *Green Earth*, where Free (my father) has a conversation with his dying mother, Ada (Alice), about being a Christian and a writer. The passage tells the story of how my father's beloved mother reacted to his dreams of being a writer and what she said to him about remaining true to himself. My father often told me how much he missed his mother and how tragic it was that she died when he was barely seventeen. But he always added that "in one way it was good" that she had not survived his father, Frank, because she might not have entirely approved of his novels. "And I'd have had an awful time explaining my vision to her or going up against her," he said, "because she never yelled at me. If I did something wrong, or she thought I hadn't been entirely honest, she'd just look at me sadly and I'd feel terrible, deep in my guts."

> "I hope to go to heaven tonight, Free." Ma looked down at her fingers where they fumbled through each other in her lap. "And, son, I'd so like it if someday you could join me there and live beside me in glory."
>
> "Ma."

"You're such a strange one. I sometimes don't understand you at all. You are not of us, really. You are not like any we have lived with."

"Oh, Ma, except that I'm too tall for doorways, I'm just like everybody else."

"You and Uncle John with your quips. No, son, I'm serious. I would very much like to have you in heaven with me and Jesus someday."

"Yes, Ma."

"At the same time, though, I don't want you to pretend to be a Christian just to please me when privately you're not. . . . Don't be a hypocrite. God hates a pious fraud." . . .

"What do you want to become?"

"A storyteller."

"What kind of reader do you have in mind?"

"Smart people, mostly. Doctors. Teachers like Professor Ralph."

"And not the average Christian?"

"Of course him too. If he wants to read them."

"What will your books look like? I mean, the nature of them?"

"Oh, like Jack London's. Or that Hardy you once wouldn't let me read. That kind."

"What a strange boy you are."

"Don't you like it that I want to be like them?"

Ma shook her head to herself. "Ada's boy a writer. Free, of Alfred and Ada, turned out to be one of those writer fellows." . . .

There was a loud call up the stairwell. "Hurry, Free! or you'll never see your ma alive on earth again."

Free was out of bed and into the legs of his overalls in one motion. He skidded downstairs. He bumped into Pa in the semidark of the living room. They bungled into the bedroom together as they fastened their suspenders.

They were too late.

The heart had stopped completely. It was done. The cheeks were losing their color. Before their very eyes her spirit rinsed out of her flesh like water soaking away in sand. . . .

Free wrote the obituary for the church paper, *The Watchman*, at Pa's request. "If you're going to be a writer," Pa said, "let's see what you can do with that."

Green Earth

Arthur Huseboe, Dad's dear friend and director of the Center for Western Studies at Augustana College in Sioux Falls, spoke next: "Fred was a newspaper reporter in the 1930s. He believed the discipline of news writing made it possible for him to be a novelist. He told me once that he could get around Sioux Falls faster than most drivers because he had been a reporter. And he wrote his own obituary as a reporter would, and I'm going to read from it because it tells the story of Fred Manfred, the reporter of Siouxland: 'When Mr. Manfred's first books appeared,

Eastern critics in New York were inclined to hail him as a new and important voice in American letters. Gradually, however, they became disenchanted with his writings when it became apparent he was not writing caustically about the Upper Midlands as Sinclair Lewis had done. Mr. Manfred was, in fact, celebrating his own country by telling his version of the truth about it. He invented a name for his country, Siouxland, which embraced the Big Sioux River watershed. He wrote about Siouxland much in the manner of a Faulkner writing about Yoknapatawpha County or a Hardy about his Wessex, in depth, with great insight in all its aspects, from Indian times to contemporary times. The range of his themes and the variety of his characters is unmatched in American Literature. Wallace Stegner in his foreword to *Conversations with Frederick*

Manfred remarked, "The inside of Fred Manfred's head is like the fairgrounds on the Fourth of July. Everybody is there, wide awake and alive."

'Mr. Manfred wrote a statement for *Contemporary Novelists*, published by the St. James Press, London:

"It has been my dream for many years to be able to finish a long hallway of pictures in fiction dealing with the country I call Siouxland (located in the center of the Upper Midlands, USA) from 1800 to the day I die. Not only must the history be fairly accurate, and the description of the flora and fauna fairly precise, and the use of the language of the place and time beautiful, but the delineation of the people by way of characterization living and illuminating. It has long been my thought that a 'place' finally selects the people who best reflect it, give it voice, and allow it to make a cultural contribution to the sum of all world culture under the sun. . . .

"The final test of good fiction rests with how well the characters come through, their reality, their meaning, their stature, their durability, no matter what the situation may be. The characters should be so well done that the reader should not be aware of plot or the unraveling of time in the work. The reader should be lost in the story. The plot should be hidden like a skeleton is in a flying eagle.

"If a 'place' truly finds voice, at last the ultimate sacred force speaks.

"And in the USA, Western American literature does this best." ' "

At the end of the funeral, Maryanna Shorba Manfred, our mother and Dad's former wife, made a short heartfelt remark about how "sweet and strong" Dad had been. And Fred reminisced about their early times together as father and son, concluding with a story of how they played pickup baseball in the yard. Then Fred placed the baseball they had played with on the coffin and sat down.

July 15, 1973
Dear Freya,

It is a cool windless Sunday and the sun is out very yellow and this afternoon Freddie is going to play in a double-header here against Slayton and before we go he and I will play a little pepper game (I throw little short quick pitches to him and he hits them accurately back to me, all to sharpen his eye before the big games) and then we'll grab a bite. All day in the sun.

Love, Dad

Finally, amid laughter and tears, I read "Frederick Manfred and the Hospital Chaplain," a true short story I'd written while Dad was dying in the hospital. And then Dad's funeral was over.

After the funeral Fred invited everyone to a public memorial to be held on October 1 at Roundwind, Dad's home in Luverne, Minnesota. He read an excerpt from my father's detailed instructions:

> I prefer a cheerful memorial meeting to be held at Roundwind. Start the meeting with music. Serve sandwiches and wine afterwards. I want everyone to drive home in a cheerful frame of mind thinking good thoughts about the making and reading of good books.

My father had also left careful instructions for his burial, which Fred did not read. Here, in part, is what Dad said:

> Coffin to be a simple knotty pine box made by a good local carpenter. (Or I may build it myself.) No tampering with body. Dress me in a gay suit. I want to be buried with my own heart, blood, guts, lymph, brains, lungs, and turds.

The funeral directors waited for the mourners to depart. They'd informed us it was "the custom around here" for everyone to leave the cemetery before they covered the coffin with dirt "because our customers don't care to see what happens to their loved one after a certain point." I had warned the directors that I might want to stay longer, and when I did, Tom and Bly and Rowan remained as well, watching the coffin disappear into the black earth. Robert Bly looked back and strode up the hill to rejoin us, and Bill Holm and John Rezmerski drifted back, too, as did others, a half dozen or so. Our son Bly stood watching with large solemn eyes, and Tom put his arm around him. Rowan wept long tears that ran down his face onto the front of his white shirt, and I put my arm around him. Robert Bly was crying, and he put his arm around me as all of us watched Dad go down into the earth, and it was not bad at all, it was good— a circle of grief and good-byes. Robert Bly said, "Your dad was an old sweetie, wasn't he?"

"Yes," I said.

"He must have had a nice mother in his early years to be such a sweetie," Robert said.

"I believe he did," I said.

December 17, 1977
Dear Freya,

Nona wrote me two days ago to say the *New York Times Book Review* will run something (very fine, she says) on *Green Earth* on January 8th. Nona told me privately that she loved the book, and: "It is truly a remarkable work, representing so much *living* experience and personal wisdom. Every page is alive with the meaning of life as it is lived."

I felt sad about it because my mother is dead and not here to enjoy having celebrated our wonderful life together earlier in this century. When I think of her I sometimes just absolutely break down in sobs of joy for having known her. She was a great person. Magnificent. And also very beautiful. You two girls are her reincarnation—yet new separate spirits all your own.

Love, Dad

A year later Tom and I were chatting with some friends at a gathering to honor Minnesota writers at the governor's mansion. One of my friends, a poet, spoke of a moment during his father's funeral when he was pushing his father's coffin down the aisle of the church. He said he suddenly realized that some kind of protection he was familiar with wasn't there. His father had put a protective shield around him, and now that shield was gone.

"That's exactly how I've been feeling," I said. "And now, somehow, I have to find a way to shield myself."

My friend smiled. "Sometimes, Freya, when I feel I don't have a shield, I pretend to have one anyway."

We didn't discuss why either of us might need or want a shield, but a few weeks later, I was sitting on our old wooden dock staring at Christmas Lake, listening to the soft lapping of waves, and gradually, overwhelmingly, the intricately latticed pattern of sun and shadow on the water rose up and entered my eyes and brain, light and dark, dancing into me. How delicate and vulnerable, this web of water and air. It was who I was. "But I need a shield to protect this fragile heart of water, sun, and shadow," I thought. And then, "No, the image *is* my shield. If only I have the courage to let it be."

Two

⟨ · ⟩   ⟨ · ⟩   ⟨ · ⟩

BEGINNINGS

"What about you, boy?
 Is your work coming along?
 Are you still making candles
 Against darkness and wrong?
 The whole thing is to blast.
 Blast and blast again. To fill the Black
 With songs, poems, temples, paintings,
 Anything at all. Attack. Attack.
 Open up and let go.
 Even if it's only blowing. But blast.
 And I say this loving my God.
 Because we are all He has at last.
 So what about it, boy?
 Is your work going well?
 Are you still lighting lamps
 Against darkness and Hell?"

Winter Count
"The Old Black Silence," Part VI

MY FATHER ROSE AT 6:00 A.M. BEFORE THE REST OF THE family and devoured three bowls of Special K cereal drenched with skim milk and topped with gobs of extralarge California raisins with seeds. (After years of eating the same breakfast, he learned these huge seeded raisins were to be discontinued and stocked up to make them last another year.) When his coffee was ready, he inhaled a soup-bowl-size cup of it, whitened with milk and three spoonfuls of sugar. He stared out the window while he ate, his sky-blue eyes dreamy, unguarded, wide open, and ready for anything, like the eyes of a sensitive child—already zeroing inward on what would become reality when his fingers hit the keys of his old black Remington Seventeen typewriter.

At 6:30 he put on his old wool coat and his tall fur hat and strode out to his tiny ten-by-fourteen-foot cabin, a remodeled white chicken coop with two small windows and a door. Inside were a plank desk, an oak swivel chair, a narrow cot with a big pillow and a little pillow and a maroon-and-gold Calvin College basketball letter blanket folded at the end of it, some shelves lined with books, and a small curtained-off closet where he stacked papers and manuscripts. Nearby were a handful of dictionaries and some files. His rugged six-foot, nine-inch frame, giant muscled shoulders, long legs, size sixteen feet, and shock of reddish brown hair made the room seem very small if you stopped by to visit. He was wearing old blue jeans, an old blue work shirt, and a long brown smock tied at the neck with wide pleats on each side.

"Daddy, why are you wearing a dress?"

"Dress? Ha! It's an artist's smock. I wear it to keep the ink off my clothes while I write. Someday, if you become an artist, you'll have one just like it."

I spied a black leather cup filled with dozens of odd-size pens and pencils beside the Remington. "Daddy, why do you need all those pencils?"

"To make corrections, Dolly. Writers need to make corrections. And to write poems, if one strikes me."

"Can I have a pencil, Daddy?"

"Of course, Dolly. Choose one. Then you can write your own books."

Morning was the quiet time. Dad hunched in his cabin, typing, concentrating, intense, "because when you write," he said, "you burn, you burn at one hundred percent; you give it all you have, and more. That's why I hate to get sick. I can't write at sixty or eighty percent. I end up with pap, just pap." He wrote hard for three or four hours, especially hard for a man who had almost died of tuberculosis less than a decade before. When he left Glen Lake Sanatorium in Minnetonka, Minnesota, after two years of complete bed rest, Dr. Sumner Cohen told him that writing fiction was too passionate and emotionally stressful a task for a man with half of one lung and a quarter of the other missing. He suggested Dad find "part-time work in other venues. Don't become a writer, or raise any children, if you want to live." This was why Dad stopped writing around 11 A.M. and took a walk to the end of the driveway to get the *Minneapolis Tribune* and then have some lunch. Afterward, he took a nap with a pillow over his head.

All morning in the summer we could hear the clacking of the typewriter keys. My sister, Marya, and my brother, Freddie, and I were instructed not to shout or fight or laugh too loud when we played in the sandbox or on the swings in the backyard. If we did, we got into trouble. *"Thwack!"* His cabin door flew open and hit the outside wall, and he jumped out roaring, face red with passion, "Dammit, I told you kids to keep quiet! I'm trying to write here!" We scattered like blackbirds, and later, if he remembered, which he usually didn't, I got scolded because I was the oldest and should have kept the others quiet. It was best to stay in the front yard, roll down the mowed hill into tall prairie grass, set up lemonade parties for my dolls, or look for bugs and flowers. But what in the world could he be doing for such a long time? When I sneaked up to peek in the cabin window—I'd better not make a sound!—he was bent over the Remington, tapping away with his forefingers, the small finger on his left hand permanently crooked because the tendons were cut when he slipped on Grandma Shorba's icy back steps and flung his hand through a window.

I didn't question how my father spent his mornings, but my friends did. Diane Pond, whose father owned a successful car repair business, and Lois Linder, a farmer's daughter, and Nemo Beach, the son of Northrup Beach, our pediatrician, made frequent comments: "What's your dodo dad doing in that old shack? How come he doesn't go to work like a normal person?" "What do you mean, 'writing' stories? Why doesn't he just tell us a story out loud?" And then, "How tall *is* he, really? Did he honestly, truly, cross-your-heart, pick up one end of Mr. Brown's Ford all by himself?"

Even as early as the age of five, I stared intensely at my father as if my *body* were trying to absorb the essence and truth of him. Did Dad's stories appear in the air above his head, where only his piercing blue eyes could spot them? Could my eyes learn to see stories, too? Or did his stories come out of the black spaces underneath his typewriter keys, clicking and clacking like teeth, spewing forth long rolling white sheets of paper covered with letters and words? How did he know which letters between A and Z to type? And later, when I was six, I asked myself: Does he know what he wants to say when he wakes up, or does it come to him during the pauses, when he stops typing and stares without looking at the whitewashed wall of his cabin? Or is he saying what God tells him? And if it's God, is it the same God who covers our hill with grass in the springtime, the God who sometimes asks me to comb his hair and the hair of his wife as I crouch near the wet earth smelling God's smell: loam, sand, stones, wheat grass, water, sun, all glittering, sweating, breathing into me? Or is there some other God inside Dad's cabin—a colorful storytelling God speaking with many voices? Or is it just Dad, long tall Dad, banging words onto the page, the same old Dad who tells stories all the time to my mother, brother, sister, and me, to the milkman, the dry cleaner, the plumber, and all the neighbors. Just our regular Dad, who leans one elbow on the top of Mrs. Linder's refrigerator and opens a beer and sips it once or twice and starts a story about the time when his father fell seventy-five feet off a windmill and survived. . . .

Although I now teach creative writing workshops, I still find it difficult to tell my students entirely *in words* how writing works, perhaps because I was first exposed to the process so young. I believe I absorbed what writing was kinesthetically, even before I learned words, certainly before I learned words to explain the process. I watched my mother write, too, and tried to absorb, understand, even memorize what she was doing. Her fascination with words and love of language matched my father's. I drank my parents in, the way I drank in the honeysuckle bushes thrusting out buds in the spring, opening their pink flowers to the sun, permeating the air with scent. The writing Dad did in his cabin suffused our house and yard, growing and changing and as natural as weather—a day-in, day-out, physical outpouring of his own blood and bone turned to black bits on a white page, which, when read, made a kind of music. His face, while he wrote, was distorted with ferocity, exhilaration, exaltation, and exhaustion. This stormy and sunny weather pattern in which I grew up encouraged me to write my own first stories when I was six.

In my nineteenth summer I came home from Macalester College thrilled to my bones because the poet James Wright had praised some poems I'd written for his twentieth-century literature class. Excited, Dad unearthed from his files my first story, "The Good Witch and the Bad Witch," dedicated to him and Mom and decorated with crayoned flowers and witches. He watched me, grinning, as the moment of the writing flooded back to me: the small chipped cherry table where I rested my elbows; the fact that I didn't like the red crayon because it was too light (I wanted dark red for the Bad Witch); the very first time I felt the loss of time and space that accompanies all deeply felt writing or work. I remembered how much more I enjoyed writing about the Bad Witch because she was more "human" and did things that were forbidden in our house. She was powerful, wild, selfish, and mean and spiteful to the Good Witch. But the Good Witch was more commanding, and she chased the Bad Witch away. Thirteen years later I felt some satisfaction about that, knowing of course that the Bad Witch wasn't exactly dead. I remarked to my father that I must have been wrestling with good and evil, even at six. And he said, "Absolutely. It's all there, full blown, the depths and the heights, the rights and the wrongs, passionate and earnest and true, and better than most of the stories I get from my college seniors."

"Oh, come on, Dad."

"No, I'm serious. I'm serious as hell."

And he gestured for me to leave so he could catch a nap.

. . .

Nap time was something he longed for after lunch, sank into, swallowed gratefully, prayerfully. No one was allowed to talk or walk or tiptoe around or even whisper. We had to lie in our beds and read books or creep far into the woods and watch animals. He slept in his cabin on his narrow cot with the little pillow over his ear and his mouth open with drool coming out one corner and wetting the big pillow under his head, sometimes snoring on the in-breaths, never snoring on the out-breaths. How could he sleep in the middle of the day? It was even more mysterious than how he wrote. This huge man with the bighearted voice that could startle you right out of yourself; this strong guy who picked up a telephone pole once, when it fell on a neighbor's car during a fire, and threw it to one side without help (all the neighbors whispered about it); this powerful man who said the frightening boys across the street would be in "big trouble" if they called me "Fre-ya Fuck-a-ma" one more time—how come he needed to sleep at all?

Kids usually forgive in ten seconds, but kids can never really forgive someone they love who naps every day. It's too boring. So naturally we woke him, by mistake and on purpose. Besides, enforced reading hours are like reading cookbook recipes you never taste. All day long I read for fun, for adventure, for joy, for lust, for profit (the kind of profit only heaven pays you). I read for the feeling of falling into things and swimming around and climbing back out. I read for the music, for the drama, for the mathematical precision, for the scientific wonder, for the philosophical wisdom, for the history, for all of these. I read eagerly—no one had to ask me to do it—letting myself go completely into other worlds, worlds just as real as everyday life but frequently so much more interesting. And both of my parents read, too, all the time, in this same intent, exploratory way, especially my father. Before dinner, if he could grab a minute, and after dinner for sure, and on weekends after chores, he lay on the lumpy brown couch in our Bloomington living room, or sat upright in the captain's chair by the fireplace at Blue Mound north of Luverne, or slouched in his blue king-size bed at Round-wind east of Luverne, with circular silver lamps blazing on each side of him like the lights of a spaceship carrying him away into the dark—and read and read and read. "The best way to be a good writer is to read," he said.

Books were everywhere in all our houses, lined up on endless, mostly homemade bookshelves in the living room, dining room, TV room, bedrooms, along the hallways, stacked on tables, desks, bureaus, and on the floor. Dad read from two or three different books or magazines each evening: four pages of Marcel Proust, ten of Charles Dickens, twenty or thirty of the latest novel by a novelist whose works he would read all of, in time. He read his favorites over and over: Chaucer, Emily Dickinson, Shakespeare, Dickens, Charles Montagu Doughty, the Wordsworths (William and Dorothy), along with all the latest novels by his truest friends and compatriots: other writers. And he read nonfiction: physics, medicine, biology, history, quantum mechanics, anthropology, and astronomy—especially astronomy. At the time of his death he subscribed to thirty-four different magazines, reading them like sweet seeded raisins added to the daily cereal of books. (Dad and Mom purchased a TV when I was in college and he was forty-eight years old, but he still read more than anyone I knew; and he wasn't too happy when we interrupted either his favorite TV shows or his favorite books.)

February 15, 1967
Dear Freya,
After I got through reading your copy of [Montaigne's] *Autobiography*, I found a copy of his *Essays* in my library,

which I bought back in 1935! A fat Giant Modern Library copy! I found it while rearranging the books on my shelves up here. I've put them somewhat in the order of their importance to me as Manfred the Western man and writer, the way perhaps my mind is arranged if you could walk through it. It feels so comfortable to me now. Because a true picture of me should include besides the features of my face and body a cloud of books floating in and out of my head.

My love to you, honey daughter, Dad

It didn't matter if I refused to read on command during Dad's naps, because I read most of the rest of the day anyway. In rural Bloomington, long before suburban sprawl and the Mall of America took over the cornfields, we drove forty-five minutes into the city and visited the Minneapolis Public Library whenever we could, and twice a month the library's bookmobile stopped at our house. Every other Tuesday I waited for the grinding sound of the long boxy green truck as it started down our graveled lane, and as soon as I heard it, I raced outside. A smiling librarian wearing a beret or a stocking cap (depending on the weather) waved at me from behind the wheel as the truck creaked to a stop. Another librarian wearing slacks (I thought they all wore skirts until this moment!) opened the buslike door and unfolded the steps for us to climb into the book-lined interior. I was the first inside, and at each visit I signed out two or three dozen books.

"Do you think they'll get mad if I take so many, Mom?"

"No, honey. That's what a library is for."

Later, when we moved to Luverne, a town of five thousand in the southwest corner of Minnesota, we visited their library every week; and several times a year we stopped at bookstores along the four-hour drive between Luverne and the Twin Cities.

When Dad and I went into a bookstore, we first checked to see if they had Dad's books, and they usually did. Then we went around looking at the other books, sniffing like wolves in new territory and rustling up spanking new titles we had to have. Naturally, we couldn't buy the books we found; we had very little money. After long deliberation, Dad chose one or two books, and with a pained expression on his face, he returned those he had to leave behind to their shelves, stroking or tapping them good-bye with his long fingers. "Write down the titles of the books you want most," he said. "We'll get them for Christmas, or you can ask at the library. That's all we can afford." Money's very dear when you live on what the U.S. government calls a "subsistence income" (the lowest amount of money you can earn and still pay taxes). It was a miracle that some of the money was spent for full sets of Mark Twain, Faulkner, Hemingway, Dickens, Tolstoy, Proust, Whitman, Melville, Dickinson, and Shakespeare. Mom wasn't excited about money going for books that could be found in the library. She had it clearly in her mind that I needed a new pair of shoes and Freddie needed pants and Marya needed piano books. Dad had it on his mind, too, but he overruled Mom. A full set of Mark Twain was more than a row of books; it was a celebration of what one writer could do in a lifetime, an example of what Dad hoped to accomplish himself. And besides, some books were so good you had to keep them inside your home for frequent reference, as if they were warm bodies, sharing the room with you, glowing with friendship and light. "As long as we have food and shelter and good books, we're OK, Dolly."

In his first decade as a writer, Dad often spoke of how his income would improve if he could "just win the Pulitzer." In fact, his third novel, *This Is the Year*, was nominated for the Pulitzer Prize in 1948 but did not win, although the Associated Press roundup of all book editors in the United States that year nominated the book as their "near unanimous" choice. Dad sometimes told how "Robert Penn Warren told me the word was they were all going to vote for me, and I would have won, but Alice Roosevelt Longworth campaigned for James Michener's *Tales of the South Pacific*." Deep disappointment on his face, Dad added, "But wait till my next novel. If I get nominated again, I'll have a better chance of winning." Dad also mentioned, less often, how Faulkner, who was "rough competition," won the Pulitzer Prize for *A Fable* in 1955, though "Red Warren was one of three judges and he told me he was voting for my book, *Lord Grizzly*."

> Pier whistled. He sang. He was overjoyed. A good year was coming again. The melting snows were sure to soak the land. Only a prolonged summer drought could rob the soil of its moisture. A bumper was on the way.
>
> This was the year all right. Sure, of course, last year had been a good year. Yes. But it had only been a sort of catch-up year, a year to lay up by, a year to catch up on all the small debts that had been mounting the four years previous.
>
> Yes, this was the year. Yessir. Ae. This year he would take a running jump at luck. This year he would pay off the mortgage on the Philosophy, South Dakota, farm. The moment the crop was harvested and the bushels cashed into money, he would rush over and plump down a wad of cash on the counter. There would be no grass growing under his feet. No longer would interest be eating him up. He was going to be a free man.
>
> *This Is the Year*

After Dad's nap, things got livelier and a lot more interesting. The writer was in a good strong mood again. He was almost always in a good mood, partly as a result of heredity, I suppose, and perhaps, at times, as an act of will. He often said he felt "grateful to wake up every morning still alive" and even more grateful he could "do what I love most— write novels." But after his nap it was time for chores, the kind a farm kid does without thinking. The huge garden had to be dug or planted or weeded, the yard mowed, fences around the nine acres fixed, the orchard grass scythed, trees planted or trimmed or chopped down, and the logs piled and split and repiled again, "neatly," near the old garage.

> He stood on the rocking, swaying frame of the plow, watching the unending slice of earth coil beneath him, crumpling, twisting, falling upside down. Roots, yellow-blue clays, air holes, worms, grubs, decayed cornstalks, strange pebbles, rusty gravellumps, lime balls, stones, mottled flecks of red and buff and black, and rusted metals, boiled up and disappeared again. The roots of Canadian thistles and wild rutabaga and morning-glory, and ragweed and pigeon grass and wild rosebush, snapped. Their stems disappeared beneath the smothering clods and wet loess veneer.
> Slowly the afternoon drifted on.
> *This Is the Year*

The garden was so prolific that we couldn't always keep up with the strawberries, asparagus, lettuce, tomatoes, green peppers, beans, peas, squash, watermelon, and cantaloupe. Around the perimeter of the garden Dad planted purple and yellow iris, white and pink and deep-rose peonies, orange tiger lilies, yellow daylilies, and many-colored hollyhocks. My mother and I planted annuals in the few remaining spaces: zinnias, bachelor's buttons, and marigolds. Many kinds of lilacs (white, double-white, pink, double-pink, purple, double-purple, deep purple, and just plain lilac) transplanted from a neighbor's country estate formed a tall, thick, uneven hedge around much of our yard; and Dad also planted apple and pear trees in the far orchard. The grape arbor he started on the hill below the house was

so successful that he announced he was going to grow cran-
berries or blueberries in the marsh below the house. Some
of the nearby farmers snickered at that idea, but not in front
of Dad.

I followed him everywhere and assisted with most of his
work, playfully lending a hand as a five-year-old, genuinely
helping by the time I was ten, reluctantly taking on even
more of the labor as I approached fifteen. We moved a small
maple tree from underneath its gigantic mother into a
sunny space where it could grow stronger. We moved fresh
sod into dead spaces in the yard. Dad put up and painted a
white arched trellis for red roses to climb on all summer, although it was "a bitch" to keep roses; they "almost aren't
worth it." When they bloomed, he sank his giant nose into
the soft petals and carried a bouquet of three roses into the
house for Mom. We weren't allowed to pick the roses—they
were too special—but I did anyway. I took them to my fort in
the lilac bushes and put them in an old glass jam jar and
gazed at them. Meanwhile it was getting toward supper, and
Dad was cursing a bit over the broken washing machine:
"Son of a bitch, Goddamn you!" His work was never done:
the car needed fixing, the toaster, the dining room chairs,
the front porch, the roof, all repaired by him to save money.
Even in the winter, leather and cloth gloves had to be
mended, as were socks, pants, blue work shirts, and jackets.
Grandma Shorba did a lot of this sewing (not to speak of
endless hours helping my mother pick and can vegetables
and fruits), but Dad, too, sat down with a thimble and
thread (and after he turned fifty, his magnifying glasses) and
darned his socks, while the blizzard groaned outside.

Summers were more exciting than winters, despite the extra
yard work, because my parents, still beautifully young and
lively (despite their bouts with TB), held big picnics or bar-

becues in our backyard, usually on Saturdays. My gorgeous, brown-skinned, dark-haired mother spent all day humming to herself in the kitchen (sometimes with Grandma Shorba's help), making deviled eggs, fruit salads, brownies, rhubarb pies, maple sugar cake, rice salads, pasta salads, and green salads galore from the overflowing garden. She taught me how to pat hamburger into flat rounds for the outdoor barbeque and how to stab cheap steak with a sharp fork to tenderize it. Once we even bought buffalo steaks, to celebrate the novel *Lord Grizzly*. She taught me how to mop, sweep, and dust the house as fast as possible (because cleaning was the boring part of the preparation) and how important it was to display lilacs, peonies, zinnias, and any other flowers the garden offered in huge vases all over the house.

Dad, his great freckled arm muscles bulging and his face red with mounting anticipation, lugged several cases of beer into the house on his shoulders. "Are we ready?" he boomed, glowing at her.

"Just one more thing. Roll back the living room rug, in case they want to dance!"

"Right. And I'll spray the yard for mosquitoes just before they arrive."

And arrive they did. Professors of zoology, history, languages, English literature, and God knows what along with sculptors, painters, architects, and writers from all over the Twin Cities parked their cars in the gravel circle outside the front door and jumped out carrying bottles and bags of food and sometimes books and manuscripts, joyfully sniffing the country air. And for hours, from late afternoon until after sunset, they trooped around our huge yard under the oaks and elms and maples, arguing and quoting poetry, drinking and gorging, hugging and kissing, questioning and answering, shrieking with laughter. And at every party I found at least one wonderful adult to talk with. Once it was Patricia

Kane, an English professor at Macalester, who asked me about the books I was reading and what I liked about them. Once it was a doctor from the University of Minnesota, who had a crush on my mother and who gave me a fascinating lecture about frogs and how to catch them in the dark. And once it was the poet James Wright with his first wife and their baby son, who told me that if I looked very deeply into the baby's eyes, he might speak to me without using words.

My favorite party took place after *Conquering Horse* was published. More than one hundred Lakota Indians from South Dakota and Minnesota showed up with drums and colorful outfits and danced and sang until dawn in honor of the book, which, they said, spoke the truth about their people. Our neighbors packed up boxes of food and drink and joined us (they couldn't have slept anyhow!). Even the horses next door stood wide-eyed with their ears pointed forward, transfixed by the drumming and the songs. With pounding hoofs they raced up and down Farmer Brown's pasture, snorting and whinnying and flicking their tails. I gave my father a push to make him dance with the rest of us, but he wanted to sit with the drummers. My mother teased him, while I danced the rabbit dance with an Indian boy named Vince. In all my years of attending parties, no get-together has ever been wilder or more satisfying to my soul.

Dad wrote his first twelve novels in Bloomington, between 1944 and 1960. Our weathered, single-story, gray-shingled rambler overlooked the Minnesota River valley and had originally been built as a ski lodge for the Chamberlain estate next door. The owners, Mr. and Mrs. Lee, charged my parents less for the house than it was probably worth, partly because they enjoyed the idea of my father being a writer. After my parents had made some payments, Grandma Mary Shorba contributed money to finish buying the house, and

Dad spent the first winter living alone there on weekdays, writing in the morning and winterizing the house in the afternoons. Mother and I moved there in the spring of 1945, and four years later in December 1949, when I was five, my sister, Marya, was born. In February 1954, my brother, Freddie, joined the family. The house was originally called Long Look, but Dad changed it to Wrâlda because one day when I was a little girl I heard our well pump making a low guttural sound in the basement, and I told my father the pump was "growling" or "talking."

"What's it saying?" he asked.

"It says, '*Rall-da, rall-da.*'"

Dad said that sounded like the Frisian word *wrâlda*, which he'd discovered could have been the source of the English word for *world*. He said it was time to change the name of the house. "I wish I'd never used Long Look," he added.

My parents couldn't afford much remodeling or redecorating, and three of the four bedrooms of the house were never painted; but the honey-colored knotty-pine living room filled with big old chairs, a couch, bookshelves, a prized stereo, and an old piano was warm with sun from the large south-facing picture window. And in the fall, winter, and spring Dad laid and lit many fires in the huge gray stone fireplace. Long before dozens of housing developments took over the nearby cornfields and woods, my siblings and I played on the river bluffs with kids from a few other houses scattered along Auto Club Road. We raised a few doomed chickens, who were either eaten by the family or perished when a weasel snuck into their chicken house and sucked out their blood. We also owned a monstrous yellow cat named Leo the Lion and a hypersensitive weimaraner we called Eugene V. Debs II, who followed our first dog, a golden retriever named Eugene V. Debs I. And, when I was thirteen, Grandma Shorba bought me a wonderful quarter horse named Chita.

I worked hard to convince Dad to let Grandma buy Chita because at first he absolutely refused, explaining that we had no extra money for food, a barn, or visits from vets. When Grandma took my side and said she'd pay extra for Chita's food and shelter, Dad became agitated, pacing up and down the living room with huge strides (five strides took him across the room). "We can't have you doing that, Grandma. We have to stand on our own feet here. You've already helped us too much already."

"But the dear girl wants the horse so badly, Fred."

"I know, I know. But we can't afford it. And that's final."

I ran weeping to my room, where I cried and moaned for hours with an ardor that astonished everyone except me. I felt as if my heart were broken. Whenever I became aware of the cutting pain caused by the thought of not possessing Chita ebbing away, I imagined galloping down a river trail on her back, and fresh tears sprang forth. At some point, I realized I couldn't cry any longer, but just then I heard my grandmother say, "That poor girl," to my father, and I decided I still had a chance. With some calculation this time, I began sobbing again, inserting a few screams of despair into my repertoire; but mostly I stuck to tears, because my father could be unpredictably aroused to fury if we screamed or yelled out of anger, and he wasn't too fond of wails of fear, either. "You have to be a man about this," he'd often say to me, when I was sad or afraid.

"I'm not a man. I'm a girl," I'd whisper, because he didn't like being contradicted.

"Of course you're a girl," he'd sputter, his face turning red. "It's just that I'm used to raising my five younger brothers, so that's why I said that to you. But you still have to stand up to things like a . . . in a manly way, you know. Be bullish. Don't give up."

This time I wasn't giving up. I knew I was testing my father's capacity for tolerance by crying for longer than a few minutes, let alone moaning and screaming, but I couldn't help myself. At least half of my groans and cries were manufactured now, but I kept on. The fact that my father had not yet told me to shut up was a good sign. Besides, I could still hear Grandma through the door, repeating, "Oh, that poor girl," and my mother had ventured once or twice, "Fred, maybe we should reconsider." "Jesus Christ!" my father muttered.

Dad wanted me to have Chita, but he truly didn't have the money. And, for the very first time in my life, I didn't care or even pretend to care about any of his problems. I had to have Chita. She was feisty, red brown, and powerfully built, with a large white blaze and unusual blue-white eyes that the neighboring farmer called "wall eyes." Even before I heard she was for sale, I had fallen in love with her hot temperament, her speed, her intensity, and the way she didn't like losing races to other horses in the Hoof Beats Saddle Club across the road at Brown's farm. I hung around the pasture, braiding her hair, petting her, and envying her owner, Dave Wall, every time he rode her; once he even let me ride her for five minutes. To me, Chita represented sweet mother-father-brother-sister-animal love and everlasting freedom.

When dinner was served I refused it. My father did not make me eat. This had never happened before. (And it never happened again.) I went on moaning.

The next morning, after staying up almost all night crying to keep the adults on edge, I startled with fear when my father suddenly swept into my room and shouted, "I'm going to let Grandma Shorba buy that horse for you. I'll fix up a stall in the tool shed. And you'll have to pay for some of the hay with your weeding money. So stop crying!" He seemed relieved and went off to write. My mother also seemed relieved and went for a walk. Grandma and I made cake in the kitchen. "I'm so glad you can have your horse, my darling Freya," she said. "I didn't think Fred would give in. But I prayed for it. Here, have two pieces of cake to celebrate. We may never see another day like this again!"

Chita became my pal, my best friend, my confidante. We rode miles together in all directions, and I developed a strong sense of independence and responsibility at a time in my early teens when it was vital. I loved being away from the rest of the family on my own, and I loved Dad's laughter when I told him some of our adventures down by the river. After each story I told him, he didn't hesitate to tell me at least two stories about his adventures with the farm horse he had loved most as a child, "that old rascal, Tip."

For a year or so Chita and I had a great life together, but at thirteen and fourteen I was not a good enough horse-woman to dictate to her and keep her well trained. She began to shy at motor scooters and trucks and occasionally bucked me off. When one of the other more experienced riders at Hoof Beats tried to give her a brief "training session," she threw him off and broke his arm. After that I was afraid of her. I hid my fear from my father for most of the winter, riding Chita less and less "because of the cold," but when spring came I had no excuses, and I had to attempt to re-train her.

Nothing I tried worked, and the fourth time Chita bucked me off I didn't bother to get back on. I led her home. My father, working in the garden, asked me what was the matter.

"I'm scared of her, Dad."

"Scared? For God's sake! She's just a horse. Show her who's boss!"

"How? How do I show her who's boss?"

"You have to put gravel in your voice when you talk with her. Like this, GIT UP! And WHOA!" He yelled so loud Chita jumped. "You try that once and she'll know who's in charge." He watched me gallop her up and down the driveway shouting "GIT UP!" and "WHOA!"; when Chita behaved, he nodded and went back to his work.

But within days Chita was bucking me off whenever she didn't want to go for a ride. Still, I didn't tell my father until he asked. "How come you don't ride your horse?"

"I can't handle her. She's too wild."

Dad sighed deeply. "Get on her once. Let me see."

Sure enough, Chita tried to buck me off as soon as I got on her, and my father was furious. He took off her saddle because it was too small for him and leaped on her back, his long legs hanging down so far his toes nearly touched the ground. Then he reached up, grabbed a nearby tree limb, broke it off, and yelled, "GIT UP!" Chita began to trot up and down the driveway. Whenever she tried to buck him off or didn't listen to his commands, he'd smack her with the branch. Within five minutes she was behaving perfectly. Dad rode her up to me and slid off. "There. She's fine now."

"But what if she doesn't behave for me?"

"She will. And if she doesn't, bring her back and I'll smack her again." Chita did behave much better ninety percent of the time.

Not long after, we had Chita bred, and she gave birth to twins prematurely. My father and I found the first colt dead under some leaves in the woods, still in its amniotic sac. "Don't worry," Dad said. "The second twin will be all right. Sometimes a mare will purposely allow the first twin to die if she knows there's to be another. She senses she doesn't quite have enough milk for two colts." A few moments later we found the second twin nearby; Chita had removed its sac to help it breathe, but it was too weak to stand or nurse. Dad carried it into the barn with Chita following. When it stopped breathing half an hour later, my father got down on his knees in the hay and tried to breathe life into its tiny whiskered mouth, while the vet we'd called stared at him in amazement. When Dad saw his efforts were useless, he bent his head over the dead creature and wept, while I hung on to Chita's neck and cried with him.

It had been Grandma Shorba's empathetic presence in the house as well as my desperate and passionate teenage need for a "pal of my heart" that permitted me to confront my father about Chita. Usually I followed Dad's rules or went along with his decisions because his physical presence was so powerful and overwhelming; I only broke his rules when I knew there was little or no chance of his finding out. He never knew, for example, that I regularly snuck across the street to buy candy bars from the store at Bethany Fellowship. (We weren't allowed to eat much candy because we had little money for dentists.) Neither he nor my mother knew that as soon as they went out to a movie, leaving me "babysitting" for Marya and Freddie, I whipped up double batches of fudge, which we gobbled until bedtime. I kept what was left under my bed for a week after, savoring it piece by piece.

It wasn't just Dad's size (which he couldn't help, of course) that scared me; it was also his big deep voice and high energy level, which at times were just too much. If I was in bed with the flu and he brought in my mail, it felt as if a tornado had blown open the door and was whirling around the room, uprooting furniture and carpets.

"Freya Girl! Here's your mail!"

"Thanks, Dad."

"No problem! I love to walk out and get the mail after a day of writing! Love it! And what a day! Sun's out! Just a few cumulus clouds in the west. Saw a mama skunk with seven babies. Stepped in some dog shit. Damn neighbor won't stop his dog from shitting by my mailbox. When I was on the farm we kept things neat. Got in trouble with Pa if we didn't!"

"Um."

"So! You're sick?"

"Yes."

"What's the problem?"

"Stomachache."

"Got a temp?"

"Hundred and two."

"Ha! Don't want to fool around with it, then. Stay down till you're normal. Better yet, stay down till after you're normal. That's what I do. Docs taught me that when I was in the 'san.' One of many things I learned from them. Never fed me right, though. Overcooked everything. I had to ask Pa to bring me farm eggs and lots of carrots! And greens! That's what saved me! Real food! Farm food!"

"Yeah, Dad, I know that story—"

"Yup. Hey, aren't you going to open your mail?"

"Maybe later. I'm not feeling—"

"Here, I'll open it for you. Might be something important."

"I really don't feel very well—"

"Well, OK. You're tired. Too bad. We could have gone to the movies tonight. Maybe see the new Paul Newman. Supposed to be a great film. I don't know much about film but I do like Newman. Did you see *The Long, Hot Summer*? There was this scene where . . ."

And Dad would stay until I either closed my eyes or asked him point-blank to leave. I was afraid to ask him to go because he always looked hurt, as if I were somehow interfering with his "helping" me get better. Sometimes, if I had the energy, I could feel myself getting angry—couldn't he see I was sick? Couldn't he see how impossible it was for me to match or appreciate his intensity? I needed one thing: for him to leave so that I could exist again, away from the roar, the power of his presence.

I was devastated when Dad decided to move away from Wrâlda to the town of Luverne in the southwest corner of Minnesota during my fifteenth summer. I couldn't speak my grief to my parents, for fear of breaking apart. I missed our home almost as much as I missed my high school pals. I had enjoyed accelerated classes in math, English, social studies, and science at Bloomington High School, and I had discovered a small group of friends who were not afraid to be smart. The lack of accelerated classes and the social pecking order of Luverne's small-town high school terrified me. I also missed the cultural events we could afford to see in the Twin Cities and the extraordinary people who visited our home: writers, painters, sculptors, professors, doctors, lawyers, and others who drove out from the Cities to barbecue steaks and drink beer in the backyard and talk politics, religion, philosophy, and the arts on our cool and breezy front porch. Although I now enjoy Luverne and have maintained friendships there, at the time I never understood why Dad so badly wanted to return to build a home on top of a low outcrop of Sioux quartzite the local people called Blue Mound. I understood that he wanted to write more books about his homeland, which he named Siouxland, but I didn't see why he had to live there.

The first time Grandma Shorba was driven up our long steep driveway to the top of Blue Mound, she remarked that the lonely hill, strewn with pink-purple boulders, prickly pear cactus, and wind-twisted oaks, reminded her of a graveyard. Dad laughed out loud, and she giggled with her breasts jiggling in a jolly way, but she was serious. She shook her wise old Slovak head while Dad explained that the land that made up Blue Mounds State Park was once a holy place for the Indians and was actually the remains of a giant mountain range that had stretched through Minnesota from the north to the south. He said he had to leave Bloomington because the Minnesota River valley was being invaded, polluted, and destroyed by factories and because he'd had his eye on Blue Mound ever since he and his father stopped to eat a picnic lunch there on a trip. "When I was a boy the place was full of Indian ghosts and wildlife, and from the top of it you could see for three hundred and sixty degrees into three states, Minnesota, Iowa, and South Dakota. So I never forgot it," he explained.

"But, Fred, all this wind up here—it takes your breath away!" Grandma cried.

"Our little quarry will protect us from the north wind," Dad said. "And I love a southwest wind!"

"Lord have mercy," Grandma intoned.

Years later Mother told me Dad had had a tuberculosis scare during the year he decided to leave Wrâlda. It was the first time his doctors had seen a "shadow" on his lungs since he'd collapsed in April 1940, sick and broke and hungry, on the streets of Minneapolis. He was taken by ambulance to Glen Lake Sanatorium, diagnosed with "terminal" tuberculosis, and left in a hallway all night because the doctors felt he would not live until morning. By the time he left the "san" two years later, thirteen of his roommates had died. And he'd met and fallen in love with Maryanna Shorba, who was also a patient there.

So when Dad's doctors again found a potential problem in 1959, he began talking about moving closer to his "homeland" of Doon, Iowa. My mother made it clear she didn't want to leave her Twin Cities "homeland" and pointed out, among other things, that Marya, a highly talented musician, ought to live closer to a more sophisticated cosmopolitan center so she could continue violin lessons. But Dad was determined to leave, and although he and my mother discussed living separately (he would take Fred to Luverne and Mom would stay at Wrâlda with Marya and me), we eventually moved to a temporary rental at the north end of Luverne while our house, which Dad called Blue Mound, was being built into a quartzite quarry about the size of an Olympic swimming pool. The house is now the Blue Mounds Interpretive Center. Buffalo heads, coyote bones, snake skins, and prairie grasses are on display in my parents' old master bedroom. Our living room, or "kiva," is full of T-shirts and books for sale. A cooler full of cold drinks stands where I sat at my desk and wrote my first book of poetry.

From the beginning, Dad's dream house was a disaster. The entire interior northern wall of the house was a low cliff of pink and purple Sioux quartzite, some of the hardest and oldest rock in the world. When we first moved in, small bits of grass and cactus were still growing in the crevices of this wall; sometimes small amounts of groundwater seeped out of it, and bull snakes found their way down its craggy face. The rest of the wood, glass, and stone house thrust out from the cliff wall and provided dramatic views of the countryside in three directions. But the Minneapolis architect, a friend of Dad's named Myron Kuehne, had not designed the house with enough practical detail, so dozens of obstacles arose in the path of Luverne contractor Marion Frakes, who had never built an atypical home from a complicated architectural blueprint. Although my father visited the site every day, troubleshooting for errors, the house was soon way over budget. To add to our problems, no one in Luverne, particularly the contractor, believed that Dad honestly had only twenty-five thousand dollars from the sale of Wrâlda to build the house. Gossip had it that Dad was a "rich writer from the Cities," who could easily afford more. Costs soon ballooned to forty thousand, and then ballooned again. Worst of all, there was no written contract. "We shook hands," my father later said in court, "and that to me was all the agreement needed between two honest men."

During the fifteen years my parents struggled to keep their house at Blue Mound, my father wrote ten novels. He'd stopped using his old Remington for first drafts and wrote all novels from *Lord Grizzly* on in longhand before typing them. Although Kuehne felt bad about the house and refused the rest of his fee, my father still couldn't pay the contractor's bill. He said Frakes had lied to him all down the line, and Frakes seemed to be saying the same about Dad. Finally, the case went to court. There were lawyers talking around our dining room table day and night, and sometimes it seemed as if nothing would ever go right again. Although the house had an incredible view, some lovely oak walls, and a gigantic fireplace, it was difficult to live in because it was never finished. The kitchen lacked half of its shelves. Although we painted the badly poured concrete floors throughout the house, they still broke up into dusty bits, and there was no point in putting good carpets over such poor flooring. The bedrooms and the bathroom were unpainted, and a second bathroom stood empty, full of spiders and an occasional bull snake. We couldn't afford to put comfortable seating or rugs into the sunken kiva living room, and during the spring snowmelt it filled with water until Dad dug drainage ditches outside the house to divert moisture. My parents rarely gave parties, large or small, and few of their old friends made the four-hour drive from the Cities to visit.

Meanwhile, my parents argued far more than they had in Bloomington, and occasionally my mother would threaten to leave. "A damn dreamer!" she would shout. "Building a house with no written contract!"

"Goddamn it, Maryanna," Dad would holler. "Frakes lied to me!"

One day in the midst of these difficult times one of the workmen didn't finish aligning a step properly, and Dad fell down the narrow rock-lined spiral staircase that led from his studio to the rest of the house. He broke seventeen ribs and had a concussion, and for a while he didn't know who he was. He was never able to finish the book he was writing, despite ample notes. "My brain can't find the thread. It's lost," he told us. He sat by the dining room table for days with his elbows on his knees, staring out the window. I circled him warily, trying not to intrude upon his desperate sadness. I had never seen him that way. Nor had my mother.

A Damned Dreamer

I go barefoot all summer long,
bareheaded,
go get the mail,
weed the garden,
stroll down to my orchard,
pick rosy-cheeked crabapples,
smell the dew in the deep grass,
toes sopping wet,
heel callouses squinching,
thinking,
oh God, how rich it all is,
summer sun,
grape juice on my lips,
hungry for hugs,

a fist in a posy . . .
please, deons,
let it last forever.

Winter Count II
August 24, 1982, Roundwind

Even now, when I recall those months in 1961 after Dad was injured, my legs shake with anxiety. My helpless parents seemed to dislike each other more each day, even resorting to telling me, separately, some of their fears and misgivings about each other; and Dad, my rock and my shield, looked half dead. He was the sort of person who always stayed in motion, who didn't give up: "I can lick this with effort and hard work." At times he was so optimistic about solutions to difficulties I wondered if he'd lost touch with reality. But, still a teenager, still his daughter, I believed in him even as I saw clearly that my mother didn't or couldn't and might have logical reasons not to. If Dad said he'd convince the judge we shouldn't pay the contractor quite so much money, by God he would do it. Or, he would half convince the judge and something good and fair would result, even if we didn't completely "win." But it was terrifying to see him sitting there staring into nothing with no sense of humor, bruised inside and out and unable to make plans, however practical, useful, wishful, or wild. For once, he and my mother totally agreed on a dark and hopeless future: we would lose the house and all our money.

He said, "The Yanktons will soon be dead. All of them. Our homeland will soon be plowed and burned away. All of it. We and our land, we are too naked. The great wagon-guns of the white man's war and the hard plows of the white man's peace have put holes in us." His face was so ashen it resembled bleached placenta. "My dreams have deserted me, even those that come only in the night. I have no dreams. When I look forward I look into blackness. When I look backward I look into blackness. I am dead ahead and I am dead behind. I have no more to say."

Scarlet Plume

Eventually a payment agreement was worked out with the contractor. To get the money, my father convinced the Minnesota state legislature to purchase our house and the land around it so that "in the future" the state could "improve" the Blue Mounds State Park north and east of us. At first Dad was led to believe we could live in the house until his death, and later he was told we could stay "for quite some time"; but in 1974 the state decided to convert our home into an interpretive center and asked us to move. In a letter to Don Davison, director of the Department of Natural Resources Division of Parks and Recreation in St. Paul, my father wrote:

March 28, 1974

My children are angry. They are in a mood to fight. I can ask them not to, but they're all over 18, and they are all individualists. My wife is bitter, furious, "wild." The worst is, I have been unable to write. I fear I'll probably never be able to write as well again as I once wrote here. I wrote by far my best books here. I had expected to be able to write here for many more years. I first expected to get life estate but when that was not in the lease and the sale terms I was reassured by Hella that it would be quite a few more years before the state could take this over—meanwhile the state needed a caretaker and who better than me? I figured that I'd get at least seven more years, maybe even more. That is why in my letters to you, and in my talk with Krona, I talked about changing the roofline, putting up a wall in the back room, painting the house, at my own expense—just as I was willing to pay for the installation of the new pump and new fabric pipes in the well. (That latter item cost me two bills. 1) $604.25 and 2) $67.41. That's a lot of money for a renter to be spending on another person's property.)

So you can see that we all were led to believe by an official, a director at that, of the Division of Parks and Recreation, that we would be living here many more years. We all feel we have been cheated, gypped, screwed by our government. It's the old story that you should never put trust in the word institution. It probably means nothing to my state that I expected to stay up here "for quite a few more years" *trying* to write masterpieces for all the world.
Harried, and in grief, Frederick Manfred

There was one amusing note to this wrenching time, though Dad found it funnier than the rest of us did. He had heard that during World War II the government had wanted to flush the Hutterites off their land in South Dakota, and the head man of the Hutterites outmaneuvered the government by asking all the Hutterite women to take off the long black dresses they usually wore and lie stark naked on the floor. When the federal marshals arrived, they found a room full of nude women and they backed off, leaving them alone. So Dad said when the sheriff arrived to remove us from our land, maybe he would resist the eviction by taking off his clothes and lying down on the floor. Years later my Dad claimed that Marya, Fred, and I told him we'd join him on the floor, while my mother laughed and said she'd just sit there and watch us.

Finally, Dad decided to move off the land. My parents separated during the move, and my mother took an apartment in Sioux Falls. "Grandma Shorba's money bought most of Wrâlda," Dad said, "which we sold to invest in Blue

Mound. So what we have left from Blue Mound belongs to Maryanna. It's not enough money, and I'd like to give her more, but I don't have it."

Dad borrowed money to buy six acres on a hill above the Rock River east of Luverne, and, as he put it, with "one dollar left" in his billfold, he borrowed more money to build a one-room dwelling into the hillside, with a garage and a tiny guest bedroom above it. Over the following years he added a living-dining-kitchen area, two bedrooms, and two and a half baths downstairs and another half bath for the upstairs guest bedroom. He also built a writing studio or "tepee" above the house, which looked east, south, and west over Siouxland. He called this house "Roundwind" because the winds come in from all directions, and here he planted a new orchard, dug a new garden, and wrote more than a dozen books during the last eighteen years of his life. Whenever Tom and I would ask him to take a walk with us at Blue Mound, he'd go, reluctantly, sadly, and reflectively. "I never wanted to give this place up," he'd say, as we strolled along, naming wildflowers. "This is where my marriage ended. I never thought I'd have a marriage that didn't go on until death."

Neither my mother nor my father remarried.

Despite endless money worries, Dad was most optimistic whenever one of his books was published. Big cardboard boxes were delivered to the house from New York, Denver, Utah, or Nebraska with one hundred copies of Dad's latest: *The Chokecherry Tree*, *The Primitive*, *The Brother*, *The Giant*, *Lord Grizzly*, *Riders of Judgment*, *Conquering Horse*. Over the years he published twenty-three novels, two volumes of poetry, two books of short stories, two collections of essays, and a reminiscence, plus his letters and conversations. After his work was done for the day, Dad got a sharp knife and carefully cut the box open; inside we discovered sleek new covers, strongly woven backs, pure white-and-black pages. Dad's big hands stroked the books. He picked one out, eased it from the box, and opened it slowly. He smelled it.

He showed us how to "break in" a book so that you didn't crack its spine. A book with a broken spine didn't "last." You held the book closed with the spine down on a table, took hold of the stiff back cover and lightly and carefully pressed it down, and then did the same with the front cover. Then, moving to the back of the book, you took hold of a few pages and gently and lovingly pressed them down. Then you moved to the front and pressed a few more pages down. You worked your way from the ends to the middle, a few pages at a time, until you reached the center of the book with two or three pages left between your fingers: the heart of the book. You smoothed the last pages down into place and closed the book. It was ready to read. You didn't peek at the ending because that spoiled the story and wasn't fair to the writer. You probably peeked at the first sentence to let your excitement build toward the moment when you would start the book. And once you began reading, you always had to give the writer one hundred pages before deciding to quit, if you quit, which you usually didn't, but it was allowed if the book was really bad. Most books you chose to read were good. You had that faith. But some were truly bad. A bad book didn't draw you in, couldn't keep you awake when you got in, or ended poorly, without reverberating in your heart and soul and without referring in any way back to where it started. A bad book was a selfish book whose author was so concerned with his or her elaborate (ever so shallow) style that he or she forgot what the book was supposed to say. A bad book was one in which the writer hadn't found a voice and sounded like anyone or everyone or something you read in the newspapers, only not as bald or as succinct or as close to life as a newspaper. A bad book showed off, pretended to have invented a new style, a new genre, or a story not already hinted at somewhere in the Bible or Shakespeare. A bad book had characters who did not come alive and greet you as if they were made of flesh and bone; or a plot that a Yankton Sioux scout couldn't follow; or a theme that shouted itself from every page and drowned out the power and the glory, the underlying melody that would sing to you for weeks and months and years after you had finished the book. There were a lot of bad books, more every year, and it was good to avoid them, but if you hadn't given each and every writer one hundred pages to get your attention, you hadn't done the fair thing. You already knew this if you had ever tried to write a book yourself.

Besides writing all morning and working as a "farmer" and repairman much of the afternoon, Dad spent hours doing research. In *The Frederick Manfred Reader*, editor John Calvin Rezmerski wrote, "[Manfred's] papers, preserved in the University of Minnesota archives, . . . show his exhaustive research and planning. The notebook for *Sons of Adam*, for example, includes a list of over a hundred terms used for various jobs in meatpacking plants. Fred made sure he knew the difference between a butt puller, a crotch breaker, and a rumper, between a stenciler and a tagger. The notebooks are full of lists of possible character names. . . . Each character is sketched out in detail, often including phrases that the character uses, and personal habits. Plots are also laid out carefully, and details of setting, and notes about the real persons on whom characters were based. . . . Sometimes [these notebooks] were completed over a very long time. For example, his earliest notes for *Of Lizards and Angels* [1992] and *The Wrath of Love* [unpublished, 1990s] were recorded in 1943, before his first book [*The Golden Bowl*, 1944] was published."

Sometimes Dad took trips around the countryside to research his books: along South Dakota's Grand River for
Lord Grizzly, to Nebraska's Republican River for *Conquering Horse*, into Canada and Minnesota's boundary waters
for *Milk of Wolves*, into Wyoming for *Riders of Judgment*,
and to the Black Hills of South Dakota for *King of Spades*.

January 24, 1967
I left Minneapolis on Friday the 1st. It was snowing.
Nothing more to tell about that day except I arrived in good
time in Deadwood in the Black Hills that evening. I sat in
the chair Wild Bill Hickok was killed in. I had a beer in the
chair. (There is some argument it is the real chair, since the
building burned down once.) The next morning there was
an 8-inch blanket of snow on the steep roads. A snowplow
and I raced to see who could get to Newcastle, Wyoming,
first. I won. Though he wrested the lead from me once. But
the pines were wonderful, like fat pocket gophers who'd
filled their pouches too greedily, and were sitting until they'd
digested some of their burden. Arrived in Denver in good
time. Had dinner with [Alan] Swallow and his wife.
I miss you much, Toopie, Love, Dad

Often, when we lived in Bloomington, Dad drove two
hundred miles to northwest Iowa, where many of his novels
are set. Later, from Luverne, he made the trip in one hour,
stopping at the town of Doon, at the Hillside Cemetery
above the river, at the farm where he was born, or at any of
the other farms his family rented.

Dad's parents, Alice and Frank Feikema, "could never
afford to buy their own farm. But they fixed up each piece of
property as if it were their own and left it shipshape, repaired, scrubbed, and painted inside and out before they
moved on." Perhaps this is not far from what Dad did each
year of his life: he gave all of his energy to a story he loved
and then left it behind for the readers—house all tidy and
finished, fields plowed and producing. And then he started

a new story, only to leave that behind when it was finished, always thinking ahead to the next story down the road, or as he put it, "to the next ball game."

> *December 29, 1986 [75th birthday party]*
> *Dear Freya and Tom and boys,*
>   That was one of the best parties I ever went to. And in that lovely house! I had no idea that the party would develop into a sort of loving roast-toast affair. And the things I heard, well, I'm still savoring them. Around next Thursday or so I'll give myself counsel about not letting it all go to my head. There's so much work to do. And you can't pitch a good game, if when you ascend the mound, you think about the glowing story describing the one-hitter you pitched last week. You've got to think about that batter standing in the box wanting to knock your block off, knock you out of the game.
> *Love, Dad*

Sometimes Dad reread a book he'd written years before and was surprised by how good the writing was. Sometimes he found problems in earlier work but felt it was too late to effectively change the novel: the moment or energizing spirit had passed. Sometimes he rewrote entirely, as when he revised his trilogy, *The Primitive*, *The Brother*, and *The Giant*, into one volume titled *Wanderlust*. Or when he revised his first novel, *The Golden Bowl*, eight times. But every book he wrote was a gift to the reader, to the artists and writers who traveled alongside him, to the "arts in America," and to the rest of the world. Regarding *The Man Who Looked like the Prince of Wales*, he said, "I hope people enjoy this book, but if they don't, I'll still write the next one." In an interview at KTCA-TV when he was eighty years old, he said, "I never know if I'm good enough, but there are moments when I feel I might even be great." When The Loft

("A Place for Writers in the Cities") planned a seventy-fifth birthday celebration for Dad, he added to a letter:

December 20, 1987

. . .

P.S. What you and Susan Broadhead have been doing about that Loft party—I sometimes feel I really don't deserve all that attention. The best is yet ahead for me. Those four novels as yet unpublished alone could establish someone with a major reputation. And *Wrath [of Love]* will top it all off. So I'm still climbing toward a plateau of excellence. (In any case, I'm going to enjoy that Loft party—at the same time that I'm not going to let that go to my head. I can't be thinking about the last good game I pitched when I've got a rough team to face ahead.) F.

Dad believed that most readers could be trusted to know what was good. No matter what their occupation or how smart they were, they would like a good story, the way they liked a warm fire in winter. Some critics could also be trusted to know what was good, but most of them were frustrated, "almost useless" writers, and you couldn't "count on them to get you up a hill in a snowstorm." You were proud of what some of them wrote, and you wanted to kill others, but they were mostly an "unhappy, unfulfilled, caterwauling bunch," and there were only a few good ones: Malcolm Cowley, Edmund Wilson, Allen Tate, and maybe John Milton from the University of South Dakota. "We're short of good critics in the 1980s and 90s, so I hope some come along soon."

Dad had tremendous respect for the daily work of other people (with the possible exception of insurance agents). Genuinely curious and humble, he asked hundreds of questions of doctors, nurses, stonecutters, carpenters, plumbers, farmers, lawyers, businessmen, teachers, and students, and he gratefully used the detailed information they provided in his books. Yet, when we discussed the potential occupations of his own children, the way Dad told it, most jobs were worthless next to writing. Or, if not exactly worthless, less magnificent. It took so much hard work and luck and true guts to even become a writer when you had a father who could not read and a mother who read mostly religious tracts and the Bible and when you came from a Calvinist community that frowned on any kind of artistic truth if it flew in the face of Our Lord. It took so much pain and fear and years of TB and slaving as a farmhand, factory worker, short-order cook, newspaper reporter, bodyguard, sparring partner, semiprofessional basketball player, and so on, to keep to the task you were truly called to: novelist and storyteller. There was so much pressure to quit and earn more money doing something more sensible and profitable—pressure from your struggling wife, your family, distant relatives, the church, the community, the state—that once you "became" a writer, you couldn't help but feel it was the luckiest and most kingly of occupations. There was nothing better to be, with the possible exception of being a composer or musician.

January 24, 1967
My Dear Freya,

What a lovely and thoughtful letter you sent me for my birthday. Not too many people are ever aware of the trials of authorship. . . .

One of the reasons I rejected teaching too, except for the short stint at Macalester, was that it got in the way [of] dreaming and projecting and imagining. And Hawthorne is right that the very toughness a man needs to keep fighting is almost in complete variance with poetic burst. Except that when you take a job and try and forget that side of you, you know an unhappiness so deep that you must either kill yourself or go back to imagining no matter what the cost. Perhaps this is a good thing. Maybe the best flowers appear on the most durable of trees. God knows, and now you, that I've had to be gnarly tough to keep on writing with all the money troubles and fights we've had in our house. Your mother almost daily keeps taunting me with the fact that I can't pay my way, that I don't even have a pot to pee in, and yet she expects me to do well enough to make the money with which to buy the pot. (I'd rather pee outdoors in the grass.) I must be a true writer because when I go to bed I think of the lovely breakfast I'll have in the morning just before I climb up to my beloved work at the desk.

My love, Dad

I believe what my father experienced as "taunting" from my mother was her expression of the desperation she felt about her family living on the edge of poverty.

When I told Dad that I felt he deserved more fame for the broad scope of his work as a writer, he responded:

April 5, 1967

I'm not too sure I want to be "famous." It would be nice to know I was famous, I suppose, just about an hour before I was to die. But before that, I don't know. An awful lot of fuss. And a lot of putting on of a friendly face when you don't care to. I do this already far too much with the little fame I now have. All I ever wanted was enough money to live simply so that I could get out The Work. I love creating. I can be completely myself, naked, or clothed, or whatever, and never have to concern myself with how my face looks as long as I write. It's like being a song, let alone writing, creating it. It's like being a bird, let alone imitating one. It's all outgo. Rise, rise, rise. Get up off the ground. Give, give, give. Outgo. Inward fountaining and outward flowing.

Anything else, getting attention, is pretty thin stuff. And of course when someone you also love kisses you and loves

you up it no longer is attention but is part of the fountaining
from the inside and is part of the flowing to the outside.
Dad

The struggle to become a writer and keep writing for more
than fifty years was so great that when Fred, just twenty,
said he was thinking of becoming an actor or a director in
the theater, Dad said, "An actor! In my opinion actors are
second-class citizens. They don't truly create, you know.
They don't write the original words." A true thing to say,
from Dad's point of view, but perhaps not the best advice
for his son, who was looking for a separate path. Yet Dad
was a genuine mentor, or father figure, to dozens of talented young people who did not know they wanted to be
writers until they met him, or who wanted to be writers
but didn't know how to proceed until they met him, or who
wrote well but had despaired of ever being published. His
students at Macalester, the University of South Dakota,
and Augustana—and dozens of other toiling writers in the
Upper Midwest—wrote him, called him, and stopped by to
find out for themselves how he managed to continue writing despite the personal and publishing odds. Many of
those who drank coffee with him, watched him, listened to
him, learned from him, are now well-known national or re-
gional writers: Pete Dexter, Michael Doane, Elly Welt,
William Earls, Dan O'Brien, Linda Hasselstrom, Craig
Volk, Bill Holm, John Calvin Rezmerski, and Joe and
Nancy Paddock. All of them know, after talking with Dad
and listening to their own hearts, what a writer is and
does.

Dad's former wife and all three of his children write,
something he often mentioned with pride. My mother
worked as a part-time, free-lance writer for years, writing
poetry, book reviews, and feature and newspaper articles, as
well as pieces for the League of Women Voters and the local

Unitarian newsletter. She also did a lot of editing and worked as a consultant for a unique magazine about South Dakota called *Prairie People*. ("I've never seen a sharper critic or a more thorough editor," Dad often said.) In his twenties, my brother wrote an award-winning newspaper column, "The Spirit of Sports," for the *Rock County Star Herald*, and then turned to plays. His play *Tongues of Stone* has been performed at Blue Mounds State Park for audiences of more than five hundred people. He has written an autobiographical account of life before and after his kidney transplant, some poetry, and a children's story and is writing another play. My sister has published a book of poems, *Original Sound*, and also writes song lyrics and music.

Dad also welcomed my work, from my first story about witches to my later poetry, fiction, and screenplays. I'd written one book of poetry (then unpublished) and was leaving for graduate school at Stanford University when he gave me the following:

> *September 12, 1966*
> *Dear Freya daughter,*
>
> Today you leave. And it is hard to take. You've become an equal friend and I find it easy to talk about anything with you. And friends are hard to come by.
>
> If I may be allowed an observation or two may I offer the following? All of us can use what you have to give. Warmth. Compassion. Light beyond brilliance. Glorious poetry said in a new way. You are your own single delightful person. Keep that. Also, don't fritter yourself away in little pieces on little people. (As I've had to do on occasion.) Little people are all right to know casually. We come from them. But we have a right to bigger warmer people and it is far better to give yourself to them.
>
> You are often wiser than I am about things I do. Use that same wisdom on yourself.
>
> You are not only a Manfred, you are Freya Manfred.
> *Love from, Dad*

Every year or so he'd read my poems and say, "This is great. Wonderful stuff! You're going to be a great writer. You're going to be better than I am. 'Course, you have my shoulders to stand on. Which means you'll be able to see farther."

> *June 29, 1976*
> *Dear Freya,*
>
> Your long poem in *New Letters* arrived, two copies. Your poem is one of the longest in the anthology. I think it's a wonderful poem. Perfect. Faultless. I sat reading it in tears of joy and memory and laughter.
>
> I'm just now getting my shoulders up to get at a new draft of a book. Am still puttering around on the yard: spraying for poison ivy, getting after musk thistles, keeping up the garden, watering the new trees.

Dad helped me look for a publisher for my first book of poetry and was thrilled when James Wright called him about the collection:

> *June 7, 1968*
> *Dear Freya,*
>
> Jim Wright just called me from New York to tell me that as one of the five judges for the Lamont Award he'd come across your poems and felt he just had to call me to tell me how great they were and that he was sitting there shaking in his room and that he hadn't read poems that were as good in ten years. "Fred, she's a marvelous poet, she's got it, it's a gift from the gods what she's got, and I want to help get them printed. . . . It is a thing that has to be done. She is great. . . . It's spontaneous with her, a pouring out of natural beauty and power."

When *A Goldenrod Will Grow* finally appeared, Dad sent a copy to Robert Penn Warren:

June 20, 1971
Dear Red,

One time, when you visited us at Wrâlda (near Minneapolis), you sat by our graystone fireplace and after awhile our little girl Freya, curious, went over and stood by you. At that time her hair was a fine copper gold and her eyes green. You looked at her for a few moments with quietly smiling eyes and then you said, "Utter." I was sitting across from you and at the time I thought, "There couldn't have been a more perfect word to catch up the look between the two of you, hers curious, yours smiling and waiting."

Well, Freya has finally "uttered" and I send it along to you.
Cordially, as always, Fred

Dad also helped me look for a publisher for *Yellow Squash Woman*, my second book of poetry, and introduced me to Paul Foreman, whose Thorp Springs Press was located in Berkeley, California.

August 20, 1976
Dear Freya,

Did you get my letter in which I told you Paul Foreman says your second volume of poems will be ready in middle September? You're more than a budding writer; you're a writer, period. You're way ahead of my schedule. I didn't get my first one done until I was 32; published, that is. You three kids will all be way ahead of me; and will be better. My fame, if there is such a thing, will rest more on that I fathered you three (along with Maryanna's mothering you) than that I authored some books. I think you're fortunate that you are with a man who will do important things in cinema, the latest of our arts. Through him you'll meet many interesting and powerful people; and he, through you, will meet many of our literary geniuses. So I can't think of a happier union. I'm glad to hear you're thinking of writing a novel. Lord, that I'd love to see. And let it all fly out. Give that old strawpile butt a good hit so all the sparrows fly out.

*Love, Pake**

I can't recall one sharply critical remark from my father in all the years of my showing him my work. Even when he felt I might be heading toward a habit of exhortation in my third book of poetry, his response was measured:

April 21, 1980
Dear Freya,

I got into bed early last night, the television programs after *Sixty Minutes* looked awful, and read your *American Roads*. I'd dipped into the book several times, you know, including reading two poems of yours Sunday at Le Sueur, but I'd never sat down and read the whole book all in one swoop. The effect is magic. I had only one little niggling interior comment. You know, what your Interior Commentator thinks? That part of you that never lies, if you've remained honest and on good terms with yourself? It is that now and then you are a bit too hortatory, so that your figures of speech start to compete with each other to see which one can go the furtherest and be the most remarkable.

When the truth is you're at your very best when your figures of speech are as soft and as shrinking as bird's-foot violets amongst a field of dandelions. Your best effects are when the metaphors are, at first glance, not noticeable. Up to now, no one can fault you. But you might take that route a bit too far in the future. I think you were doing it too in *The Follower* as compared to the first novel you did. I once was about to take that route myself, in the first draft (unpublished) of the trilogy, and with a rigorous aboutface I revised the trilogy and ever since have been on the watch for it.

Your "American Roads" poem is the best. Full of good pictures, moods, passions.

---

* *Pake* is the Frisian word for *grandfather*, although my father had no grandchildren when he first began using the term to close some letters.

I took note of Dad's comments without worrying about them. His prime piece of advice was always, "Tell everyone to 'fire and fall back.' And don't listen to me, either. Write for yourself first." In fact, my next poems were as "soft as bird's-foot violets," with fewer "figures of speech," perhaps because when I was writing about the birth of my sons and raising them, I had little free time. My poems emerged quickly amid breast-feedings and sleep deprivation or not at all, so they became smaller, softer, shorter.

> *May 28, 1984—Memorial Day*
> *Dear Freya,*
>
> Thanks for handing me those poems about Highfield. I've read them all three times and each time they get better. I think you've deepened as well as become more liquid. Really a vast improvement! If it is true that Overlook [of Viking Press] is going to reissue your *American Roads* in quality paperback, they're sure to publish these new ones. There was a time when I was afraid you were going to become a mite too hortatory. But looking at these poems, and looking back, I can see where I was wrong. You and Warren and McGrath are the best poets going now.
>
> Am writing every day. Am on page 1525 (at the end of this morning). Goes very well.
> *Love, Dad*

Besides warning me not to listen too much to anyone regarding my work, Dad also stressed staying in touch with one's "lizard." The lizard is the one who knows, when you meet people and stand nodding and chatting with them, what's really going on "deep down." The lizard knows whether others are *truly* happy, unhappy, in a rage, lying, telling the truth, about to die, or incredibly alive, even when people don't know what they're feeling themselves. And one of the best ways to stay in touch with one's lizard is to pay attention to one's dreams.

Dad and I often shared our dreams. Once, in 1967, I told Dad I'd dreamed he was on the cover of *Time*, and he replied:

April 5, 1967
Dear Freya,

It's almost a cohinkeydinkey (co-hinky-dinky?) that you should be writing me about your Manfred-on-the-front-page-of-*Time* dream and that I should be writing you about enjoying your dreams and nightmares. Cultivate your dreams and your nightmares. They're often the best part of your life. It's a sign, if your private Dreamer will give you this, of being a creative person to be able to remember them afterwards. Most dead people alive today can't remember their dreams because their Dreamer knows they are not worthy [of] knowing about them. What I usually do, if a dream or a nightmare awakens me in the night is to hoist myself up on my pillow a little—not too high because then the Dreamer in you becomes alarmed you're paying too much attention—and relive the dream or nightmare. Be thoroughly scared or moved or whatever by it and yet with a little sideways smile enjoy it too. Nor must one take on a superior air about such dreams. The sideways smile must be one that is mostly serious. . . . If one allows one's Dreamer to have the freedom to dream anything it or he wants, and then is circumspect and polite when it or he offers them to you for you to look at, you will dream more and more "out-loud," so to speak. And the more you do this the tougher and healthier you'll be all your life.

Your, Dad

A year later he sent me a dream he said helped him survive:

1-7-1968, Sunday 1 P.M.
Dear Freya,

The night after you left, I had a strange dream. I was walking through a desolate city. Brown brick houses were

fallen in, brown cobblestone streets were torn up, bulldoz-
ers were at work everywhere trying to straighten out the
streets and alleys, the bulldozer operators all had sad faces
and they would shake their heads at each [other] at the in-
tersections. The only thing living that I could see were rats,
mice, and little urchins with blown-up potbellies. After
awhile I was aware that a little fairskinned child (a girl, I believe) was following me. Soon the child asked me at my
heels, "But, Dad, where are the streams, and the trees, and
the green hills?" "Let's keep walking," I said. "Maybe we'll
find them somewhere." We walked and walked. Presently we
came to the outskirts of the crumbling brown desolation.
Soon we saw little valleys. The valleys deepened. One of the
valleys began to run with a stream. Then the trees and the
green hills came into view. "There they are," I said. "I'm so
happy, Dad." "What's your name, child?" "Freymanfred." At
that point I woke with a great sweating start. It took me a
long while to find sleep after that dream. It was a sad and a
beautiful dream both.

Monday morning. More.
    It came to me where that dream came from. From that
painting of yours over the radio in the music room. I had a
good chance to study that painting as I lay there with my
broken arm, in various kinds of lighting, daylight, lamplight,
moonlight. (This was while you were in the back room with
your flu.) Remember how Marya would put on a bunch of
records after I'd go to bed? I'd lay listening and musing on
the little yellow girl standing on the leaf of the great blue
flower, looking love thoughts into the flower's heart. Her
hands were of the perfect size to hold the shy flower's petals
open and her feet were exactly right to stand firmly on its
green leaf. And her body, lithe, slim, was also just right to
make the flower feel important. In a word, that painting is
perfect. Some day I want that, if you care to give it to someone. Though I must warn you that it is priceless. It is a perfect masterpiece of realism and fantasy combined. You are

not only a great poet. You are also a great painter. And I long
for the time, soon now, another year maybe, when you can
go at it full time.
Love, Dad

I became suspicious because my father's response to my
writing was always, "This is terrific! I love it!" Surely some
of my work was not as well written as the rest? I began to
question him: "Dad, did you really like everything in the
manuscript? Is there some poem you feel is less effective, or
a poem you prefer?"

"No. I like them all. It's all as good or better than any poet
writing today. You may not get it all published now, but
someday, after you die, you'll be discovered and you'll be one
of the best this country has. Keep that in mind."

"I can't wait that long, Dad!"

"You have to. It's all wonderful work."

"Surely you exaggerate?"

"No, I don't. My work's the same. It's all quite good, better than some of the critics think—each book different, some
very different, from what I wrote before. Taken together as
a whole body of work, which is how you must take all artists'
works, my stuff is all wonderful."

Dad read almost all of my poetry, but he only saw two of
my five novels. He especially enjoyed the first novel, *Lily
Nye*, written in my twenties and praised by editors, but
never published. *Lily* was my "life story" from birth to age
fifteen, featuring Dad, Mom, Grandma Shorba, my school-
mates, my siblings, and my dear horse, Chita. I tried to con-
vey my youthful fears and dreams in this novel and re-
experienced much joy and anger as I wrote; so when I asked
Dad to read it, I was worried how he might feel about my
descriptions of him. Would he mind, for example, that I
tried to capture his arguments with my mother? (Contrary

to what is supposed to be the typical male-female quarreling pattern, my mother argued logically, albeit loudly at times, working her way carefully from A to Z, unless she finally blew her stack and then anything might happen, including some stomping and door slamming. And my father argued, just as loudly, along the lines of his gut feelings, refusing to be logical, sticking throughout to the emotional content or one particularly upsetting image or issue or *thing* that had gotten to him, which might also, finally, include some stomping and door slamming.)

Here's a description of my parents from *Lily Nye*:

> Lily snuggled under two quilts in her bedroom, reading *Don Quixote*. The Don was a marvelous new acquaintance. He reminded her of a grown-up Tom Sawyer. But Sancho was her favorite. She chuckled when he pricked the Don's balloons with his matter-of-fact observations. Sancho's blunt remarks reminded her of Mom's comments on some of Dad's schemes. When she read the section where the Don and Sancho discuss farting, she laughed aloud. Her raucous shouts rose above the blizzard's howl.
>
> "Is it *that* funny?" Mom hollered.
>
> "Which part are you on now?" Dad yelled.
>
> "It's the part about farts."
>
> "Oh yeah," Dad said. For a few minutes Lily could hear him chuckling to himself as he remembered the fart dialogue.
>
> "Oh for Christ sake!" Mom said.
>
> "What?" Dad said.
>
> "Oh, just your barnyard sense of humor, that's all."
>
> "Not at all," Dad said, still chuckling, "it's Cervantes' humor. Hilarious. Read it once and you'll see!"

This is Dad going to bed:

> Dad was tired, so he said good night early, and ambled down the hall toward his bedroom. He was wearing his short gray

nightshirt. Beneath it his long bare legs hung out like an ostrich's. He arrived at the big black space behind the door to the bedroom, and suddenly—a ball of bristling yellow fur dove out of the black space, flying directly toward Dad at knee level. Twenty claws dug into his thigh.

Dad roared. He jumped back, smacking the kitty with one hand. She hung on, teeth buried in Dad's white, goosebumpy leg, her green eyes aflame. Dad had to bend down and unlatch her back claws. She drew out her front claws herself, and threw herself down the hallway like a streak of light.

Lily and Penelope stared as the kitty skittered to a stop in the living room, her hair standing on end, her tail lashing. A strangled sound came from Dad's end of the hall. They peered around the corner. Dad sat on the floor with his back against the wall, laughing so hard that tears dropped out of his eyes.

"I'd hate to see what would happen if she was all grown up," Dad choked. Tears dripped off his chin. "She might drag in a buffalo."

And here's Dad and Mom going to the movies:

Lately Lily didn't like much about Dad's looks. (She used to think he was the handsomest guy of all.) Everyone stared at him. He was too tall and wore lumber jacket shirts and jeans. And his voice was as loud as a jack hammer. He was always shouting or talking: "Hi, Merve! Hi ya, Joe! Great day, Burt!" Shout, shout, shout. Everyone turned to look, startled by his booming laugh, or uprooted by his swearing. Whenever Lily went to the movies with him, she avoided taking a place in line next to him until the last minute. As soon as Dad paid for her ticket, she skipped back out of line and ran for a seat in the back of the theater where Dad would not sit. She would die if the kids saw her with him.

Once she agreed to sit with Mom and Dad during *The Long, Hot Summer*, starring Paul Newman, and she wanted to strangle Dad most of the evening. Before the movie began, Dad yelled hello to everyone he knew, and said, "This is my daughter, LILY," and "Yup, she's really growing UP there," and "You betcha, she's a ripe one," all the time patting Lily on the back with his big hand. The kids from her class at school stared and nudged each other. Dad wasn't wearing a suit like the other fathers, and he laughed more freely, and he kept announcing his opinions when no one asked for them.

Dad was introducing her to the town banker when the lights went out. Lily sat down with relief. During the movie she sat with her head below the edge of the back of her chair so no one could complain that she was too tall. Dad loomed above her, so tall that some people behind him had to move over one seat.

Lily's school friends started laughing and hissing and burping during the love scenes. To Lily's surprise and horror, Dad turned around and shouted, "Stop that farting around!" in his gravel voice. There were a few loud whispers about "farts" and "farting around" from the kids, but they quieted. Lily knew they would tell everyone else in the school what Dad said.

"What a plot! Call that a plot?" Dad said, as the movie ended. "By God, I could write a better plot with one hand tied behind my back."

"I thought it was GREAT," Lily protested.

"Terrible. And terrible acting. Unrealistic. That's not how a guy would talk when . . ." Dad pointed out the bad parts of the film to Mom as they marched out of the theater. Lily dropped far behind so Dad wouldn't ruin the movie for her by talking about it in such detail. Didn't Dad realize how wonderful Paul Newman was? Lily's bones ached for Paul's face, his eyes, his battered lips, his agony . . .

Dad told me he laughed until tears ran down his face when he read my descriptions of him, especially the chapter in which the father remodels a toolshed to make a barn for Lily's horse and then has to quell the wily bucking animal by riding it around the yard until Lily can mount it without fear. But his "favorite part" was the moment when Lily boosts her terrified Grandma Shorba up on her horse for a ride:

> "There you go, Gram!"
>
> Gram hunched over the saddle horn. "Yez-us Christ-us. God help a poor woman!" Gram's face was white. She stared down at Lily. "Don't let her run away with me!"
>
> "I won't. I'll lead her, Gram."
>
> Gram clutched the saddle horn and sat stiffly as Lily led Flick once around the driveway. Gram's gray-flowered dress fluttered up and down in the wind, and her knee-high nylons rolled down to her ankles. Lily could see the blue varicose veins going up Gram's leg.
>
> "God be merciful," Gram muttered, as they came slowly back to the garden and Lily stopped Flick.
>
> "How's that, Gram? You did great!"
>
> "Yez-us Christ-us, God preserve us all."

Dad and I often swapped stories about Grandma Shorba. He would tell a story about her, and then I would tell one, back and forth, until tears of joy and sadness rolled down our faces. Dad told me he planned to put this bright, earthy, five-foot, one-inch Slovak, a graduate of St. Margaret's Academy in Minneapolis, in a book someday, and said he'd already used "a few pieces of her." But he said, "You know, Freya, you've got her in *Lily Nye*, and I don't think I could ever get her the way you have. You inhaled her when you were a girl, and now that you've grown up, you've breathed her onto the page."

Perhaps my father didn't mind my sometimes critical descriptions of him because they were written from the exaggerated point of view of a hypersensitive, hormonally challenged fifteen-year-old in the throes of a teenage identity crisis. But I think it's more likely that he accepted them because they were mostly on the mark, but couched in the form of fiction. Dad was very sensitive to any amount of criticism in real life. Even a passing comment from a friend would sting him for days. "Now why do you suppose John made such a remark to me?" he'd ask my mother, his giant face full of childlike hurt. "I just want to know why, because it's not true, and dammit, he knows it." As a child or a teenager, I hardly dared to criticize either of my parents. Their strong reactions were sometimes scary.

When I openly criticized my father a few times, I was in my twenties, at an age when almost everything I remembered or observed about my parents was placed under a magnifying glass and scrutinized in my passionate, sometimes successful and sometimes misguided efforts to change and improve my then lonely life. When I spoke to Dad about some frustrating aspect of his behavior—mostly the fact that I wanted him to talk less and listen more—he either turned beet red and stared at me in bewildered shock and then changed the subject, or he became angry and defensive. Once I recall him shouting, "Well, if you don't like the way I talk with you, I won't be your father anymore!" I smile at his bluff even as I write this, although at the time it frightened me and made me shut up. I now see him as if he were one of my adolescent sons, caught between being a child and an adult. When dealing with critical outsiders, Dad was reserved and clearheaded and showed an honest effort to understand the other person's point of view. He remained calm and "fatherly," no matter how nutty or difficult the circumstances. But when I disagreed with him or criticized him, he reacted with the volcanic energy and deep primitive passion of a teenager—sweet, brilliant, amazingly self-sufficient, romantic, dreamy, and full of love—but terrified of making any mistakes: both desperate to please and determined to stand his ground. He was at times unable to *see* me as a separate person, a not very powerful person really, so intense was his defensiveness when criticized. Around me, his reaction to most of life was always boyishly heartfelt, an electric response to things that shocked, stunned, or overjoyed him.

I was worried when Dad said nothing about my second novel, *The Follower*, which I shared with him in draft form in 1978. I thought perhaps he hated it but was unwilling to say such a negative thing to his own daughter. I began to feel he wasn't entirely happy to think of me as a novelist. He seemed to prefer either my poetry or my role as a poet, because when I talked about my novels, he changed the subject immediately to his own novels. Then, a few years later, I overheard him praising *The Follower* to several of his friends, and I realized he had suffered from a lack of critical acclaim and public attention to his own work for too long and had no heart for worrying about my publication problems as well.

I believe part of the lack of attention to my father's work as an American novelist was due to his reputation as merely a "Western writer" or "regionalist" rather than as an author who spoke to the American soul or could legitimately reach a broader audience. His lack of prominence was also due to his almost total adherence to a singular vision as a chronicler of the Upper Midwest, a region he celebrated without apology or satire. Nor did he have a lot of time, money, or energy left after writing, raising kids, maintaining a house and garden, and reading vast numbers of books and papers to travel to New York to meet with agents, critics, editors, and other writers to push or publicize himself. He was a maverick who didn't intend to take suggestions on how to earn more money by writing to fit the sometimes condescending preconceptions of East Coast literati. He also refused to follow dozens of suggestions from members of his childhood Christian Reformed church to cut out the earthy aspects of his novels, and he would not add a "revolutionary or proletarian" ending to *The Golden Bowl* when a "left wing" press in New York said they'd publish the book if he did. Although he had "a liberal bent," he said he'd heard enough preaching in the church to ever want to preach about the left wing in any of his books. "I don't like to adhere strictly to any one political or religious group," he'd sigh. "They all think they know the whole truth and that's not possible."

In their introduction to *Frederick Manfred: A Bibliography and Publishing History*, Rodney J. Mulder and John H. Timmerman address the question of the place of the western writer in American letters: "The curious fact remains that while novelists like Manfred, Vardis Fisher, A. B. Guthrie, Jr., Walter Van Tilburg Clark, and others are commonly mentioned as 'major' American writers, and while they have survived well the critical scrutiny of academic insight, their popular acclaim, with few exceptions, has remained uncommonly small. Few of their works reside for more than a brief spell on the best seller lists—and when they do, they appear there as a strange cousin who slipped in a back door and crashed the party." Mulder and Timmerman suggest that several of Dad's works "bear clear evidence" of the traits of "classic, enduring literature": aesthetic excellence (being a work of fine art), universality of meaning (applying to peoples of different times and places), anchorage in history and a life experience (having something significant to say about the time), and spiritual significance (revealing the quest for human and spiritual meaning). They conclude: "We are left, then, with the curious question of why such works should be studiously ignored by the literary marketplace of the eastern publishing world . . . [which], for the most part, has been lukewarm to regionalists in our century, and has been slow to recognize that in the particular one might see more clearly the universal significance. 'Siouxland' has an odd ring to it. Something like Yoknapatawpha."

Mulder and Timmerman suggest that the "publishing world has been guilty of negligence in recognizing the peculiar spirit of [western] art. Western literature is often mythic in the sense in which Mircea Eliade uses the term in his *Myth and Reality*. Such literature begins in the physical thing in order to seek the primordial thing; the real meaning behind the fact." Max Westbrook, a professor of literature and friend of my father's, further explained this bent toward open-ended structure in western literature in his essay "Conservative, Liberal, and Western: Three Modes of American Realism": "In Eastern realism the conscious mind is primary: in Western realism the unconscious mind is primary." Mulder and Timmerman expand on this idea: "The eastern mind is analytic; the western speculative, open-ended." The result of these different orientations, Westbrook concludes, is that, "emphasis on the conscious mind causes the Easterner to be discontent with what strikes him as an irresponsible structure in much of Western art."

My father was often accused of using this sort of open-ended structure by eastern reviewers and publishers, and Mulder and Timmerman quote Dad's response in "The Novelists of Western America": "So we starve as we write, and our children wear hand-me-downs, and our wives go mad looking through wish-books while lying in bed under a pile of buffalo robes in a cold house." But Dad, who kept a list of the novels he intended to write up to the age of ninety-one tacked to the shelf in front of him as he typed, did not swerve from his dream and intention. As Mulder and Timmerman aptly explain: "Early on, the genius of [Manfred's] writings attracted a potentially wide press. He determined, nonetheless, that he was going to craft his own peculiar vision by his artistic means. The opportunity for the big dollar has been available more than once, but the opportunity sometimes stood at odds with his particular artistic voice and vision. The bibliographic history of Manfred is not only, then, a story of who sold or bought what; but it is also the story of the pursuance of an artistic vision."

Part of this vision was seen in my father's decision to change his name. In 1952, eight years after he'd begun his career with the pen name of Feike Feikema (Fy-kah Fy-kah-ma) at the suggestion of the publisher of his first book, *The Golden Bowl*, he decided to call himself Frederick Manfred. By then he'd written six books, one of which had been nominated for a Pulitzer Prize, but he took the radical step of changing both his pen and his legal name because he was worried that Feike and Feikema had been mispronounced from the beginning, and he feared that his book sales were being hurt. I still recall the day Dad drove me home from second grade and told me my name was no longer Freya Feikema but Freya Manfred. When I asked him why we were changing our name, he said that we were not changing its deeper meaning. He explained that "Feikema" meant "Fredman," or "Manfred," an Anglo-Saxon name he liked because it meant "man of peace" or "peaceful man." Unfortunately, the change left many readers confused or lost. I met a number of writers at the MacDowell Colony and at Yaddo in my twenties who were startled to find out that Feike Feikema had not died or stopped writing in 1952 but was alive and well and now calling himself Frederick Manfred. Similarly, readers who enjoyed the work of the new novelist Frederick Manfred rarely sought out or purchased the books of Feike Feikema.

The times in which Dad wrote also affected his career. When he began writing, the country was eighty percent rural, and when he died it was eighty percent urban and suburban. Even movies had shifted from Westerns to urban dramas, high-concept love stories and comic book action adventures. Observing this trend, in his later years Dad lived with the simple hope of at least getting each and every book published, no matter how small the press, how unfair the contract, or how little the money. John Calvin Rezmerski, in the introduction to *The Frederick Manfred Reader*, writes, "After the publication of *Eden Prairie*, Manfred was increasingly finding it difficult to place his books with the commercial publishing houses. His most loyal audience was aging, and younger audiences were not discovering his books, or were not finding them 'relevant' when they did discover them. (Again, the 'Buckskin Man' stories were exceptions). Often, Manfred's novels were not discovered because they were not available widely enough. I believe that one of the greatest misfortunes in twentieth-century American literature is that *Green Earth* did not achieve great distribution, reach a wider audience, and gain more critical attention. It is a book whose like we have not seen, and may never see." (When *Green Earth* was published, Dad's fellow artists and some professors from universities where he had taught nominated Dad for the Nobel Prize for Literature for the fifth time.)

Also during this period many reliable publishers were swallowed by conglomerates, who expected greater profit margins for the books they produced. Unless they could predict stellar sales, they wouldn't publish, and Dad's later novels, poorly publicized and frequently unheralded by critics, sold far less than the "bean counters" required. Cookbooks were more profitable.

October 28, 1977
Dear Freya,

It was good to get your comments on *Green Earth*. I sometimes am more concerned what you think than an Edmund Wilson. You read things with your whole being. That little Freya who was quite critical of Jehovah when I was reading out of the Bible is a hard one to get by. Tell Tom, by the way, that Crown had an option on *Green Earth*. When you sign a book contract it really is a two-or-more book contract. When I signed *The Manly-Hearted [Woman]* contract it automatically meant Crown had first-look rights at *Green Earth*. But I would have gone with Crown in any case because of the editor I had, David McDowell. Also, Crown is now one of the top houses in New York. It is one of the few independently owned or privately owned houses left. Knopf, Random House, etc., are now owned by holding companies who really don't give a shit about literature. Crown is sort of hard-hearted too, but at least they have a great editor there.

Since my father wanted to get all his novels out, he may even have thought my work was some slight competition for the piece of publishing pie every fiction writer in America wants. Conversations about my striving for publication inevitably led to concern about his own dwindling career.

What happened in Dad's books was frequently connected to what was happening in the rest of his life, or the life of his family. When Tom and I left for California on our wedding day, he sent a note and one hundred dollars along with us:

October 2, 1976
Dear Freya and Tom,

Here is a little gas and food money for you while the two of you look around for a new nest to settle in. With it I send my love and my best wishes for a happy life together.

When you read *Green Earth* someday (hopefully a year from now) you will understand why I give you this particular sum of money, instead of say seventy-five or a hundred-twenty-five. The reference will come in the first part of the book.*

My father had no daughter he could give such a gift to, but I do. So a Frederick to a Freya-Tom gift follows upon a Frederick to an Alice-Frank gift.

Good luck and God bless. I think it quite appropriate that the two of you who should be feeling "on top of the world" should be getting married on a place that the Indians regarded as "the top of the world" near Eagle rock, Blue Mounds.

Love, Dad

I got along best with my father when I learned to speak my thoughts and feelings without being asked. Our relationship didn't work as well if I waited for him to inquire about my life. Once, when Tom and I visited Dad at Round-wind during the third month of my pregnancy, for four days Dad didn't ask me how I felt or mention that he was going to be a grandfather: he talked about black holes, the Hubble spacecraft, the genius of Eudora Welty, the novel he was writing, and each of the students in his wonderful writing class at the University of South Dakota. Feeling even more passionate than usual because of my pregnancy, I fell into a silent rage. Finally, Tom, white-faced and protective, asked Dad why he didn't seem at all interested in this major event of our lives. Wide-eyed, Dad replied, "Well, for Godsakes— I didn't know you wanted to talk about it!"

During my fourth month of pregnancy, he wrote:

March 2, 1980

How is the big event coming? Your flesh novel. I think of you every day and wonder how you and Tom are making it. If you're over your cold. If Tom took that special writing job.

* In *Green Earth*, my father's grandfather gives his son, Alfred, and his daughter-in-law, Ada, a wedding gift of one hundred dollars.

Has your book arrived yet? Did you lose any dirt in all that rain? And so on. Every day. Remember I'm thinking of you both every day.

Much love to you both. Dad

And during my eighth month he wrote:

June 7, 1980
Dear Freya and Tom,

I had a dream the other night in which I got the message about the coming twins. The one that your doctor identified as a boy is going to be a center but the other one is going to be a point guard. A center moves a little slower than a guard, especially a point guard, and that was why he could nail the center but not [the too] fast-moving guard. Very funny. It will be fun to see if that midnight augury turns out to be correct or not.*

Love, Dad

It was not difficult for me to jump from poetry into novels in 1978, even though by that time my father had published more than twenty books. I wrote my first novel, *Lily Nye*, because I needed to hear my story (how I survived) told in my own words, not the words of my brilliant mother or father. I didn't think about publication. Then I leaped into *The Follower* because I fell in love with the main character, Vidonia March, and I began to dream about being published so that other people could meet her. My third novel, *Wife's Tale*, was nearly impossible to begin because the second came close to being accepted so often, and I had to shed many tears of regret over the "miscarriage" of my "book child" and not seeing it in print before I could move on. I

* Dad's "midnight augury" has partially come true. At eighteen and six feet, five inches, both our sons play varsity basketball as centers for the Blake School.

shed more tears before I started my fourth novel, *Move Heaven and Earth: The Kidnapping of Jonathan Oakes*, because no one accepted the third novel either, although many praised it. "Publishing is getting harder," Dad said, to console me. "I'm not sure they still know what a good book is." *Move Heaven and Earth* was the "most commercial" and most highly praised of all my novels, but it, too, was never published.

It never occurred to me not to write four novels because Dad had already written so many. I didn't feel profoundly competitive with him—the river running through me was uniquely mine, and I drank from it too greedily to concern myself about where my father was slaking his thirst. But I often felt directly competitive on a more superficial level because Dad was, with incredible effort, finding small publishers and less commercial houses to take his books.

"I wish I could get just one novel published," I said to him.

"Me, too. One for you and one for me," he said. "But don't stop writing, Freya."

"But not even one of my novels is published! At least you have twenty-five novels to look back on."

"I don't look back. I want the novel I'm writing now to get out."

"I know. But, Dad, maybe I'm not good enough."

"Freya, sometimes I don't know if I'm good enough either. Nights especially, when I'm alone in bed. But I make up my mind that when I get up the next morning I'll decide *then* whether I'm good enough. And by God, after a cup of coffee and a look at the sun coming up over the fields, I am good enough."

I hear the same determined, unpretentious tone in what my father wrote to me on the flyleaf of *The Golden Bowl*:

"Dear Freya, I hope you won't be too disappointed in your Papa's first book, born the same year you were born." Ten years later in his best-seller, *Lord Grizzly*, he wrote, "Honey, I hope this story is interesting to you, and not too sad, but it is a true story." And in *Wanderlust*: "To my dear Freya, in awe and respect for the new age coming which you will help to make." And in *Eden Prairie*, one of his greatest small novels: "To my daughter, Freya Manfred, humbly, to one who will run a longer mile, and in better time. Your father." In the midst of being humble, he was often confident: "Nothing wrong with wanting to be number one. Nothing wrong with being number one. Nothing wrong with being sure of yourself, or even arrogant. Some people are marvelously good at what they do. These are the real kings and queens of nature. These are the true artists, and they should not suffer fools. I'm talking about a kind of permissible arrogance, Freya, and it's OK to cultivate that in yourself—everyone needs that now and then." I can still see him: red-faced and smiling and encased in self-engendered joy, genuinely welcoming me, and everyone else, to the world of writing, a hard but worthwhile place to be.

> *3-29-1970*
> *Dear Freya,*
>
> There are probably some 5,000,000 natural born brilliant people at any given time in our present society and every one of them without working too much at it can present brilliant things. It is easy to be brilliant, and to seem brilliant, if you're born brilliant. But it is another matter for a brilliant person to come through with something simple and moving and profound. It's the difference between an Einstein and a complicated-sounding professor of mathematics. It's those mental leaps, jumps, that count. Intuitive making beyond learning. Not the reasoned out things. In

fact, I can't think of a single new idea that has ever been arrived at by sheer rational thinking. It is true that a good
mind has to be exposed to a lot of rational thinking around
it for it to make those jumps. Nevertheless, it is still the
jumpers who make it go. And the curious thing is, once
you've become a jumper, you can hardly go back to being
just a rational person.
Love, Dad

After *Sons of Adam* in 1980, Dad barely managed to stay
in print with the poems in *Winter Count II* in 1987, and in
1989, the essays in *Prime Fathers*, the *Selected Letters*, and a
novel, *The Flowers of Desire*. The University of Oklahoma
Press published *No Fun on Sunday* in 1990 and *Of Lizards
and Angels* in 1992, but neither sold well. Dad's last agent,
Al Eisele, was unable to sell *The Wrath of Love*, finished in
1992, and never saw *Black Earth*, the first draft of which
Dad stopped writing six weeks before he died in 1994. Although Dad said the manuscript was unfinished, in fact it
ends beautifully with the death of his father, a conclusion
that exactly parallels *Green Earth*, which ends with the
death of his mother.

After Dad died, Fred and I found letters in his file from
the 1980–87 period when nothing he wrote was published,
letters in which he asked sponsors for money to finish his
kitchen at Roundwind or to buy food and gas so that he
could keep on writing. He had a small income from teaching creative writing one day a week at the University of
South Dakota and later at Augustana College, but those
stipends didn't cover what he needed—and he didn't need or
take much. That a writer who had contributed so much to
his country and culture was reduced to begging between the
ages of seventy and eighty is tragic: a proud man asking for
money from those who have millions because the books
come first, before pride.

March 2, 1980
TO Freya Feikema Manfred Pope
FROM Frederick Feikema Manfred VII, her father but more her friend
SUBJECT I managed to live through the February doldrums. The last week of the month I totaled up my tax things and then sent them on to the accountant. Didn't have as good a year as the one before on just earnings. Otherwise very good. But I look with more misgivings toward the summer months. I don't see how I'm going to live through four months. Once I'm into October, I'm all right—provided USD hires me again. There's a rumor that the new busybody Vice President wants to drop all extras, and that includes the writer-in-residence program. But I won't give up without a bit of a struggle. After all, I got to here; so I think I'll get to there.

Nor did he enjoy reviewing books to earn extra money:

March 2, 1966
Dear Freya,
    I spent the whole damned day reading and writing a book review. This doesn't count the reading I'd done on the book over the weekend. The book, *Disinherited* by Dale Van Every, is a good one, non-fiction, but I don't get enough return out of it to do it. I hate reviewing. It's the exact opposite of creative writing. Instead of exploding you're deploding. (If there is such a word.)
    Tomorrow I must get at making out several applications myself for help. . . . I do hope you don't give up exploring all possibilities for next year in some school. But don't feel too depressed over the fact that you are fundamentally a creative person, not a critical or academic person, because the truth is you are one in a million.
    Love, Dad

When our sons were born, Dad scraped up some money and flew to California to see them. (My mother came, too, on another flight.) Full of joy, Dad held one diapered baby in one hand and the other on his lap. He exulted: "Now we have *two* firstborn boys to continue the Feikema line. For six generations the Feikemas have had a firstborn boy. I was born first, so I became Frederick Feikema the Seventh. Then you came along, Freya, a firstborn girl, and stopped the line of firstborn boys. When your brother was born after you and Marya, we named him Frederick Feikema (Manfred) the Eighth. Now, just one generation after you became the firstborn girl, you gave birth to *two* firstborn boys—twins!—the firstborn of the firstborn for nine generations! Wait and see, Nicholas Bly and Ethan Rowan will have dozens of children, and we'll have more Feikemas and Manfreds to take over this country and run things right. These two boys will be president and vice-president for sure!"

Six months later, I asked Dad to come and visit his grandkids again, and when he said he didn't have the money, we sent him a Christmas present, a check to cover one round-trip flight to California. The check was returned, slam-bang, in the next mail, and a few weeks later he came out, on borrowed money, I suppose. He told us to leave the boys with him overnight, and I protested. "They'll wake up in the middle of the night, and then you'll be in trouble! Six-month-old twins don't just lie there, Dad. It's a lot of work—you won't get much sleep."

"I've been tending babies all my life," he said. "I took care of all five of my brothers. It'll be fun. Go!"

So we went, our first date in nine months.

When Dad visited us two years later in 1982, Rowan and Bly found a new game: climbing up Pake's broad back and sliding down his chest and belly and long legs to the floor. Then they'd race around behind him and start all over again, cackling with glee, while he talked about his latest novel and his teaching. Actually, Dad was low that trip. His knee hurt, and he still hadn't had it replaced with a metal knee. He wept about Fred, who had discovered in November 1980 that he had kidney failure as a result of a congenital ureteral defect. Fred started dialysis in April 1981 when he lost total kidney function and got a kidney transplant in July 1981, which failed a month later. (Fred received a second transplant, this time successful, in 1992.) Dad was also upset by my sister's depression and anxiety, which caused her to be hospitalized several times. For the first time in his life Dad looked his actual age, instead of younger, and I began to wonder (for the first time in *my* life) how long he'd live. His lips were gray, his eyes pained and weary; he limped badly and sometimes startled when the children squealed. But he had always taken care of his health, and he continued to stick to good meals and at least one nap a day. He had knee replacement surgery and kept writing until he gradually regained his good spirits and went on for another twelve years with vigor.

A writer who nearly dies from tuberculosis when he's in his twenties and spends two years in a tuberculosis sanatorium, where he watches a succession of thirteen roommates die, has to develop and keep strong habits to get his writing done. Here are a few of my father's rules:

1. *Don't party or drink alcohol on weeknights. Your work will suffer the next day.*

   July 19, 1968
   Dear Freya,

   I, personally, do frown on the use of any narcotics, drugs, etc., unless medically prescribed. There is just no excuse, none at all, for any use of pot, nicotine, LSD, the like, and only goddam fools indulge in it. Liquor there might be some excuse for, as it has food value. The others have no value of any kind, and they probably damage one. In my house there will never be any pot parties; and I don't like it when any one smokes in it. Copulation, yes. Swearing, yes. Truth-telling, yes. Hearing voices, yes. Loud smacking over food, my god yes. Burping, maybe. Cries of joy, oh dear sweet father yes. *Dad*

2. *Resist visitors on weekdays, except Friday. Talk is great fun, but it takes energy, which must be saved for writing.*
3. *Stop writing after three hours, or sooner if you get tired, so you'll have something left for the next day.*
4. *Nap every day.*
5. *Answer letters and do errands on Saturday.*
6. *Rest on Sunday. This means no church except the great outdoors, lots of sleep, the Sunday paper, waffles or pancakes, and maybe a visit with a friend.*
7. *Keep your meals simple: cereal for breakfast, a slice of bread and an apple for lunch, a slab of meat and some vegetables for dinner. After dinner, try ice cream or bread with jam piled on it an inch thick. Candy's OK on Sundays, but you better cache it in some high place only you can reach or one of your kids will ferret it out and eat it.*
8. *Keep your weight down. It's better for your knees, and besides, your body is the greatest miracle you'll ever possess.*
9. *Exercise every day: walk, or use a ski machine, dig a garden, clean house, keep moving.*
10. *Don't keep a dog or a cat. Dogs demand too much attention, and cats belong in barns where they can catch mice. If the neighbor's cat comes over to eat your mice, that's a gift. It's a pleasure to watch a good mouser work and maybe have her sit in your lap, too, if you're outside reading in the sun.*

11. *Don't get into an argument with a close relative. If someone starts up, it's best to fall silent.*
12. *There's no king or queen worth crossing the street to see. Writers and thinkers are the true aristocracy.*
13. *Find time to be quiet and alone.*

And the most important thing on Dad's list: don't whine about how hard it is to write. Several of my talented friends were the children of well-known authors who grumbled and complained endlessly about the tribulations of writing. As a consequence, my friends made up their minds never to write a word themselves. But Dad never complained about how hard writing was. He left for work excited. He returned tired but happy. Writing was a gift and a blessing, and he was lucky.

> Each day was a gift. Each day came wrapped in sparkling morning sunlight.
> For most people, days are all alike. They forget that they are presents from the unknown.
> But Eric knew they were gifts, all of them. One by one they came, and he knew they would not come again; that this day he was having, this one short spurt of time, this one was the last of its kind; that once it vanished into evening's melancholy sunfall, it was gone forever.
> He caressed them and called them each a name.
> This one, this day, he named "a golden drop."
> The next one, this day, he named "a water drop."
> The next one, this day, he named "a golden drop."
> They were all new and different names, they were, because when a day died at sunfall he forgot it sleeping; and waking, found a new one and named it the best name he knew, "a golden drop, a water drop."
> *Boy Almighty*

Dad gave speeches to make extra money, but the older he became the more he hated it, unless he could visit an exotic place like Hawaii or Banff, Canada, and take an extra day or two to explore. He couldn't afford a longer visit, although he didn't say so. Instead he said, "I want to stay home and finish my novel, but this speech is a necessary nuisance."

October 12, 1988
Dear Freya,

Three weeks ago last Sunday I became very ill with the flu. Spent a week in bed—interrupted twice by talks I had to give which I'd agreed to do and for which I got needed good money. Each time I rose from the sludge and phlegm like a Neptune rising from the sea to give the talk and then collapsed again. I'm still sniffing a little. But the temperature and pulse are normal again.

Love, Dad

He enjoyed writing festivals and workshops more than speeches because he could meet and talk with his literary friends. He enjoyed PEN (the International Association of Poets, Playwrights, Editors, Essayists, and Novelists) meetings in New York so much, on his infrequent trips there, that he'd describe them in detail: setting, atmosphere, speeches, parties, food, and especially the people. He'd leap to his feet to imitate how this or that writer stood or spoke or walked and quote what he or she said. After his imitation of John Updike, it was easy for me to instantly recognize that author on a crowded sidewalk in New York—something about the way he inclined his head and moved his face and hands, though the last time I'd "met" him he was six feet, nine inches tall and was wearing size sixteen buckskin boots with fringes.

As he got older, whether he traveled for business or pleasure, Dad always mentioned "losing precious writing time." But in the last decade of his life, he especially enjoyed the Marshall Festivals at Southwest State University, where he joined writers Tom McGrath, William Stafford, Carol Bly, Robert Bly, Meridel Le Sueur, and others in riveting and

Frederick, mother Alice (holding Abben), Edward (back), John (front), father Frank, and Floyd Feikema, 1924. Henry, the youngest, was not yet born.

My parents' wedding day, October 31, 1942 (left to right): Floyd Feikema, Frederick Feikema, Grandma Mary Shorba, Maryanna Shorba Feikema, and Floyd's wife, Adeline

Dad and me with Eugene V. Debs I at Wrâlda, September 2, 1945. "How tall is he, really? Did he honestly, truly, cross-your-heart, pick up one end of Mr. Brown's Ford all by himself?"

Mom, Dad, Marya, Freddie, and me at Wrâlda, 1954. The dining-room window looked east over the river valley.

Dad's writing cabin as it appeared in October 1994 at Roundwind. It had been moved twice, first from Wrâlda and then from Blue Mound.

"To me, Chita represented sweet mother-father-brother-sister-animal love and everlasting freedom."

Frederick Manfred at Blue Mound, 1973. "At first Dad was led to believe we could live in the house till his death."

Dad, me, Fred, Mom, and Marya at Blue Mound in the summer of 1973

The Feikema men, 1973: Henry, Abben, Frank (Pa), Edward, Floyd, Frederick, and John

was escorted by Dad on my wedding day, October 2, 1976, on top of Blue Mound.

Blue Mounds Interpretive Center, August 1994. "During the fifteen years my parents struggled to keep their house at Blue Mound, my father wrote ten novels."

Dad with Bly and Rowan Pope, Ojai, California, 1980. "Now we have two firstborn boys to continue the Feikema line."

At Blue Mound, August 1991. Dad wrote to me: "You've become an equal friend and I find it easy to talk about anything with you."

At my father's funeral on September 10, 1994, I read a story about his conversation with the hospital chaplain. On the plain pine coffin are Dad's peace pipe and the baseball he and my brother, Fred, had played with.

Fred and I and about two hundred others shared many reminiscences at Dad's memorial service in October 1994 at Roundwind.

Rowan, Tom, me (holding Whiskers), and Bly on the deck of our home on Christmas Lake, November 1994

widely attended workshops. He also enjoyed the Western Literature Association conference each fall:

> *October 12, 1988*
> *Dear Freya,*
>   It was fun to get your card right after I got back from Eugene, Oregon, where I went to the yearly meeting of the Western Literature Association. I presented a plaque to Max Westbrook there. I also sat next to Ken Kesey at the head dinner table. He'd known about me and me him. We had a great time talking, and finally took off talking about quantum mechanics and poetry and writers and wives and teachers. He was in the same class under Stegner with Larry McMurtry, Wendell Berry, and Don Berry. He told me in an aside that *King of Spades* was the only Greek novel in American literature. (I think that was a bit of "high" complimenting in the excitement of the moment.)
> *Dad*

Dad often mentioned visiting with Luverne High School's creative writing and English classes. He was delighted to show the students where and how he worked and crowed with joy because they kept him up "far too late" asking questions. He also looked forward to visiting Calvin College, his alma mater, Macalester College, where he taught in 1949, and St. John's University, where he could visit J. F. Powers, whom he greatly admired. "What a brilliant writer that man is! He should write more! I wish he didn't have to teach so much."

Dad didn't want any writers he admired to "waste time" teaching, selling books, editing, or doing anything other than what they were put on earth to do: writing.

> *March 1, 1981*
> *Sunday, sunny, clear, lovely out, lazy inside*
> *Dear Freya and Tom,*
>   Have been catching up on another Minnesota (new) novelist, Jon Hassler, *Staggerford* and *Simon's Night*. Hassler

was born in 1933 and it wasn't until a few years ago that he decided, as a teacher, to start writing novels. He's quite good and in some ways I like him better than Sinclair Lewis. He writes quietly, with plenty of irony and very sharp dialogue. His plotting too is good. Occasionally he pushes the irony a little bit too far. But it is rewarding to read him. I'm to give a talk at Saint John's at Collegeville late in April and I'll meet him there along with J. F. Powers. I met Hassler once before and I liked him. Tall man, grave, a little smile.

June 7, 1980

Had, in general, a good trip East. Spent an afternoon with Larry McMurtry in his Booked Up Bookshop. Bright quick fellow. Wrote *Leaving Cheyenne* and so on. Also writes lots of reviews. He knew about you, Freya. He writes both in Texas and in Washington, D.C., two weeks in one place and two weeks in the other. Sells nothing but $1000 books, so makes good money with little public traffic. Then . . . I visited John W. Huizenga and wife Juliet for lunch and a whole afternoon. Very sharp tiger kind of mind. . . . [He] questioned everything about the artist and "his pretensions." [I] of course questioned the CIA and its pretensions.

Love, Dad

Sometimes Dad wondered why "those guys" teaching in the English department at the University of Minnesota didn't "pay more attention" to his work. "I'm a Minnesota writer who's been writing and publishing for half a century. Don't they care to ask me any questions about the body of my work? What sort of Ph.D.s are they?" He used to say they were "only interested in literature if it came from the British Isles with a faint sneer on its lower lip" and he was "better off without them." (The university's Creative Writing program, whose faculty included the poet Michael Dennis Browne, did invite Dad to read there. Dad also gave his correspondence and memorabilia to the university's archives and sent copies to the Center for Western Studies in Sioux Falls, South Dakota.)

After my father and mother separated in 1975, I often wondered how Dad felt about spending most of his time alone. For the first ten years, he assured me he liked his quiet days and nights, "where joy visits me once more." But during his last decade, he said, "I'm sometimes very lonely here, but I can't seem to find the right woman to stay with me." Then he'd launch into a long description of his latest "crush." His crushes became younger as he grew older. At first the women he liked were older than I was. Then they were my age. And finally, they could have been my daughters. I was glad their presence in his life sustained him through long dreary winters and decades of writing, but I wanted my father to be happy in a single relationship or even a marriage with one special person because that's what he claimed *he* wanted. (I wanted my mother to find someone she loved as well.) Meanwhile, I wasn't interested in long gossipy stories about his dates, especially as each woman got younger and (in my opinion) less complex or interesting. It upset me that he didn't seem to tune into these crushes as real people but related to them as glorified muses; he kept the young women on such high pedestals that he didn't seem to realize that some of them cared about him, but others "used" him, partly in the hopes of advancing their own writing careers. Tom observed that Dad probably didn't want to live with anyone that badly—he wanted a source of inspiration. And I observed that his books were like family and friends to him, and writing them took up much of his emotional life.

Whenever Dad took off on a long discourse about his latest girlfriend, I listened politely for a while and then changed the subject. It was years before I worked up the courage to say, "You know, Dad, I don't want to hear too much about this. It makes me feel a little uncomfortable. I'm your daughter, and it feels odd to hear a lot about your attraction to this girl."

"Oh," he said, startled. "Well, I think of you as a friend, I guess."

"I know," I said, "but I can't entirely get past the daughter part."

"Well, I'm not saying anything against your mother, you know. Maryanna and I aren't married anymore, and we are both allowed to have other interests."

"Oh, it's not that, Dad. I don't see much comparison between your latest love interest and our mother. You were married to Mom for many years, good times and bad, and you raised children together. What you have with this young woman is more like a crush."

"You think so?"

"Yes, I do."

"Well, it's interesting to hear you say that. Maybe you're right. But that's not so bad, is it?"

"No, if you feel good about it."

"I feel great. I sometimes don't think Freddie approves, but I can't help that."

"No, you can't. Fred's feelings are quite natural, I'm sure. But it's your life, not his."

"And you're sure you don't mind my looking for a girl-friend?"

"Not at all. I'm very glad for you. I want you to be happy."

"Well, I want me to be happy, too."

During the last ten or fifteen years with my father, I never brought up past differences, difficulties, or problems. I didn't believe in dragging out old grievances for two reasons. First, I had moved well past my early years; Dad was no longer scary, overwhelming, or too "big" for me to handle. I'd taken a lot of time to think about my parents' behavior to determine which aspects of them to keep within myself and which to discard. I tried not to repeat some of their patterns with our sons, but I made plenty of innovative mistakes of my own as a parent. I saw no point in commenting on their possible "errors," especially since there was no longer anything they could do about the past and when, in fact, they were not the same people they once were, any more than I was the same person. And second, both of my parents had a certain innocence and goodness that is rare in this world, and they usually meant well.

In September 1974, when Fred was twenty and I was thirty, we conducted a taped interview with my father at Blue Mound. Here Dad spoke of the writer's loneliness and touched on how he viewed his favorite books.

FRED: "A writer spends much of every day alone with his work and his desk and his typewriter. What makes a person choose that writer's solitude as a way of life?"

FREDERICK: "Maybe it's because I'm part bear, grizzly bear [laugh]. Grizzlies, male grizzlies particularly, *like* to be alone a lot. Well, I don't know that they like to be alone a lot, but they do spend a lot of their time alone. After they've had their love affair with the mama grizzly bear they wander off by themselves, and the older they get, the more they are alone. But perhaps more importantly, if you're going to do anything creatively, whether it's in architecture, or writing novels, or sculpture, you can't be spending your time in the presence of other people, if you want to really explore your ideas. You have to spend a lot of time alone to know what you really think about things. The voices of other people, when it comes to decide what you want to do, are terrible intrusions, and you don't want to hear what they have to say. And actually when you're so-called solitary, you really aren't alone. Your head's full of all kinds of voices, including your own private tone voice, or what I call your own personal tone. And you can't hear that tone if you're in the presence of people too long and too often."

FREYA: "Which of your books do you feel most proud of—that is, which book would now be your best friend?"

FREDERICK: "I always say I never have a favorite, and I like them all like a father might like all his children, but, you know, if you examine that remark carefully, there sits a little smile in that response. Or certainly, if not a smile—a smile indicates you know better—if not a smile, then a slight dishonesty, because without any question a parent does finally have a slight favorite over another. You like them all, but there's one that you feel—not that you're prejudiced or that you tend to be a favorite-picker, but rather that some physiognomies, some kind of souls, get along with one kind of soul better than another. You're either more chemically in tune or more instinctively attuned to one person more than you are to another, and that's something you can't help. You might find this with your children, too.

"I feel that two books came out of me like a dream. I don't understand how they ever came out of me. And interestingly enough, both, in my eyes, came out practically perfect. I did some rewriting and cutting and so on, but . . . the outline . . . the shape, was mostly there. And that was *Conquering Horse* and then the one I wrote last summer, *The Manly-Hearted Woman*. When I was writing these books I had a very odd feeling, as if I wasn't [here]—I was here in a sense, I enjoyed my breakfast and I enjoyed working in the garden and so on—but that was just sort of like touching, like a bird touching the ground before the next hop in which it took off for another good solo flight for three or four or five hours.

"As I say, I came closest to being in a dream when I was writing those two books. I don't mean a nightmare, but I mean a real beautiful dream. You know how the reality of the dream is far more real than anything you do in real life.

The content in a dream and your actions in a dream are tremendously overpowering. They can make you shiver and quake and wake up in a sweat . . . a kind of reality as if every nerve in your body has been touched by an electric charge, which is something you rarely get in life except, say, at the moment of a near accident or the moment when you hit a home run or something like that—at these moments you become fully alive. But in the dream you become *terribly alive*, and it's in that sense that those books seemed to come out of me, out of that kind of a strange, otherworldly—I don't like that word *worldly* there—otherworldly kind of living. The other books had moments, too, but not like those two."

In 1991, Rick Hauser, an executive producer at KTCA-TV in St. Paul asked me if I'd interview Dad for *Portrait*, a series about well-known Minnesotans. The show featured two fine interviewers, but Rick thought it would be interesting if a writer interviewed her writer father. During this interview Dad again spoke about "tone."

FREDERICK: "When I was a very little boy someone told me that the wires between telephone poles were carrying voices. That's when we first had our telephone. See, I was born at a time where there were no telephones, no TV, no records, nothing. There was just plain country living. Then the telephone came in and that was a miracle to me, that voices could go over wires. So I used to run over and stick my head against the poles and see if I could hear anything, and yes, I could hear a buzzing and a humming, but I couldn't hear any voices. And then I went to trees to listen to trees, and I learned that the bigger the tree and the harder the wind, the more they start to talk. It's only recently when I was up in the North Woods here some years ago, just before I wrote *Milk of Wolves*, that I found out that those great red pines and those great white pines have symphonies in them. And it's not unlike the whales making symphonies in the ocean, very similar to that sound. So since then, when I want to listen to my own things I keep waiting for my tone to show up. If you sit alone long enough you hear your own tone after a while, not only your heart beating or your breathing, but something else . . ."

FREYA: "Do you have . . . what is your tone?"

FREDERICK: "Well, actually, I've been trying to capture it and get it into my writing. And I hope it shows up in there somewhere . . ."

FREYA: "Is it better not to know your tone?"

FREDERICK: "I don't want really to know too much about it, except that I know it's there, and I sort of vaguely hear it, and I know when it's coming off my fingertips into the type-writer or into my pen. It's like I told you about this friend of mine, a young woman poet. I knew her socially. I knew her in her clothes. And it was always interesting, and she was lively. Her letters were fun. But then I finally read all her poems sitting down one night and there, suddenly—something beside the really fine lines in the poetry and so on—suddenly the tone of her, the Eve of her, started to show up in there, which I hadn't noticed before—the real woman—the old Eve came in there: that's what I mean by tone. And if you read me . . ."

FREYA: "But tone is not just old Eve and old Adam . . . or is it?"

FREDERICK: "No, it's deeper than that. It's the sound . . . [Pause.] Maybe it's the sound of eternity trying to speak."

In the last segment, Dad spoke of his own death.

FREYA: "Do you think any more about death at eighty than you would have at forty or twenty?"

FREDERICK: "No, I just know it can happen any second. It can happen right now. But I've had a big, full life, and, as I go into it I'd say, 'Well, let's have a look at it. Wonder what it is.' And there'd be no regrets. I've had more than my share of life. Why should I ask for more? But if it's given to me, by God, I'll take that, too."

FREYA: "So if you had a picture of yourself as you move into death, what would you be doing?"

FREDERICK: "I hope with my eyes wide open to have a good look! And if you understand the history of where we came from—the trilobites. Half a billion years ago, one of the trilobites developed some cartilage, and that cartilage became a backbone, and we came out of that. All the other trilobites died. So whatever we get is really rather wonderful, even if it's kind of sad. That's the way I look at that. It's better than nothing. Even pain is better than nothing. Pain means you've been there."

FREYA: "If you could have been anybody else, other than yourself, who would you be?"

FREDERICK: "Well, Socrates. If there is a heaven, I'd like to make sure that I land in his compartment. [Laughs.] You know, if there are different compartments or provinces there, I hope I land in his province. The same way with the great Greek dramatists: Aeschylus, Sophocles, Euripides, and Aristophanes. Aristophanes particularly. I like him because he's so sarcastic. Oh, and Chaucer. I'd like to meet him and see him again someday. I often think about him."

FREYA: "You've read and studied about the solar system for fifty years, and you're fascinated by quantum mechanics. Why?"

FREDERICK: "To understand things better. These men— Bohr, Heisenberg, Planck, and Einstein—they're getting at first principles, and they explain an awful lot of stuff we didn't know before, and I'm curious about that. I like to know. So I welcome all those findings. It enriches my life."

FREYA: "Do you think the human race will 'make it'?"

FREDERICK: [Pause] "To what? The sun eventually is going to burn up the hydrogen, and it's going to become a huge helium ball, and then it's going to start expanding, and then it will suck in the earth and so on, and then it will explode, and then all the particles that make up the whole solar system will explode out—you know, like you see all those penumbras out there—and then other suns will suck them up, and so all those metals and stuff will be reused somewhere else. We're made up of metals that were made up in another solar system that exploded a long time ago somewhere. So in that sense, the human being will make it because they'll be reused. [Smiles.]"

FREYA: "And how does it feel that even the writing will go then?"

FREDERICK: "Maybe there'll be some other way of communication in that new rule that's being made up—like we have movies that came in recently. You know, maybe some other way of doing something. I don't know. I haven't thought about that. Maybe I should write a novel about it and then I would know."

Three

⟨ · ⟩   ⟨ · ⟩   ⟨ · ⟩

THE END

When the Riders of Judgment come down from the sky
And the Big Boss fans wide His great circle drive
And critters come in from low and from high
And critters rise up both dead and alive—
Will you be ready for that Roundup of Ages?

Riders of Judgment

I FIRST KNEW IN OCTOBER 1993 THAT DAD WASN'T going to be alive much longer. We had gone to visit him at Roundwind for a few days, and one evening while Dad, Tom, Bly, and Rowan chatted and watched the Vikings football game by the fire, I stepped out for a rambling walk through the gray-green, rust-rose prairie grasses, thrashing and hissing in the autumn wind. Returning an hour later, I walked down a path Dad had carefully mowed under the apple and pear trees south of the house, and suddenly something *spoke* to me from inside the wind's near-winter voice, a wave or a ripple overwhelming all other thoughts—and I knew I'd be walking on Dad's hill the next October, but I'd be walking alone because Dad would be dead. An actual visual image of my father and myself in the present, and my father absent from my side within a year, came into my mind, along with the words, "This is his last October."

"How can you think such a thing?" I said to myself, as my eyes filled with tears. I hurried back toward the lights shining from Dad's stone house, scolding myself, "You're all wrong, Freya. At eighty-two he's got plenty of energy. He says he plans to stay alive until he's at least ninety-one. He's tacked the list of books he still intends to write to his bookshelf above the typewriter. Sure, he's getting older and he probably won't be the same person by next October because he'll need some more help in his house, but he'll certainly still be here!" And I bargained: "Maybe he'll have a few little strokes, but he won't be dead."

But even as I persuaded myself that my gut feeling was wrong, another part of me knew what I had sensed was true.

And that part of me began to grieve. And worry. How would I handle Dad's death?

All that winter, from November through March, I felt panicky when I took long walks alone, especially when I had a bad cold or if the sun was setting. I sometimes felt I could not breathe or that I might die out on the winter roads, and I asked my husband to take walks with me. I've always been a lone walker, like my father, because it gives me a chance to walk into my writing and my dreams; but now I felt utterly alone. Abandoned. I kept saying to myself, "For Christ's sake, he's not dead yet! If you're this frightened now, what will you feel when he actually dies?"

In time I saw that some of my breathless fear came from a sense of rootlessness and displacement because Tom and I had been trying to sell our house for two years, and, when we did, we had to move our family twice in six months. I also realized Dad represented stability, fortitude, hearth, and home. The oldest of six boys, he'd lost his mother when he was seventeen and his youngest brother, Henry, was two; so he became a second parent to his five siblings. He became the rock, the leader, the general, the king—the one who protected the house, the farmyard, and the family, including its rites, rituals, and morality. He carried this stance into his marriage and fathering. When I was very young and he and my mother argued, it was she who sometimes said she had to leave; Dad stayed, built a fire, did the chores, and paced the floor until she returned. Mom was a softer, more tender presence, but it was Dad, sometimes too strict, sometimes gentle and afraid, who said firmly, when I asked him, that he *would never* leave me. As I grew older, it was sometimes hard to feel I was independently moving along with my life, since when I was small he had so much power and control over family decisions. Unlike many fathers of his era, he took an active interest in us when we were babies because he genuinely got a kick out of younger children, while my mother said she was more drawn to teenagers, partly because they could carry on an intellectual conversation.

Within a few months after my "vision" of Dad's death, I suggested to Fred that if he planned to move from California back to Luverne, he might as well do it soon and not wait another year. I also told a few close relatives and friends in the spring of 1994 that they might consider visiting Dad soon, that he was doing well, but. . . . Waring Jones had other plans until late summer, so he saw Dad just a few days before he died. Uncle Henry, on the other hand, spent several wonderful days with Dad in June, driving around northwest Iowa looking at the farms where their parents and other relatives had lived. Uncle Henry had always remained close to Dad, sometimes viewing him almost as a father figure as well as a brother. Before Uncle Henry died of cancer, just twenty months after my father died, he told me that they could talk about anything together and that Dad was his best friend.

Tom, Rowan, Bly, and I had a good visit with Dad and Fred a week before Thanksgiving at our temporary apartment in Minnetonka. We ate lamb and drank red wine, and Dad told stories and joshed with Fred and the boys. He talked about how much he was enjoying his work on *Black Earth* and how he hoped the book before that, *The Wrath of Love*, would be accepted soon by a publisher. For more than a decade I had been privileged to read his books in rough draft before publication, including *No Fun on Sunday*, *Flowers of Desire*, and *Of Lizards and Angels*, but I excused myself from reading *Wrath* because it was the story of Dad and Mom's marriage. I explained to Dad that I didn't want to get riled up by reading a story I'd lived through once already, and I didn't want to find myself in disagreement with Dad's "view" of his marriage or taking sides or feeling sad about the past.

"But it's not like that, Freya," Dad said, as persuasively as he could. "A lot of wonderful things happen amid the pain. And I'm very fair to the wife's point of view. It's not a one-sided book. Not at all."

"That's OK, Dad. I think I'll wait a few years."

"It's a marvelous story," he said. "You're really missing something!" And we both laughed at how he was promoting *Wrath* so enthusiastically to his own daughter.

"Too bad you're not your own salesman," I said.

"Ya, when would I get the time?" he answered, shaking his head. "I should have been two people. Twins. Or brothers, like Vincent and Theo van Gogh."

He did look tired, more so than usual. When I drove him over to sleep at Uncle Henry's house, he was perfectly satisfied to be chauffeured through the Minneapolis traffic, but he was clear as a bell about where to turn for the short cut to Uncle Henry's.

In February 1994, we spent two days with Dad because his brother Edward Feikema had died at the age of eighty in Doon, Iowa. Although Dad had lost another brother, John Feikema, years before, he was shocked and upset by the death of the brother closest in age to him. "Ever since Ed died, I've been having nightmares. Eddie was my closest playmate and I miss him. We were eighteen months apart. I wish I hadn't looked at him in his coffin. I can't get it out of my head. And then I had to go to the graveyard and watch them lower him into that frozen black hole. I shouldn't have done that. The image of that black hole haunts me so." During this visit Uncle Henry said Dad had forgotten that Marya accompanied him to Ed's funeral and then wondered how she got there. He asked if Dad often forgot such things, and I said I didn't think so. I suggested that the shock of Ed's death might have caused a small stroke or memory lapse during Ed's funeral. Uncle Henry said that was probably the case, and we dropped the matter.

In March, we spent another two days with Dad during the funeral of Katherine "Kash" Vander Kooi, a dear family friend. Several people, including Ben Vander Kooi, Kash's son, told me Dad was behaving oddly. After Kash's funeral, Dad offered to drive some of her relatives to the graveside ceremony; but as they drove along in the funeral procession Dad became impatient and said he was going to "pass that damned hearse" because it wasn't "going fast enough." Tom and I felt bad when we heard this, but since Dad behaved in a lucid and intelligent manner when we were with him, we assumed the sadness of Kash's death following so soon after Uncle Ed's might have caused another small stroke. I remember watching Dad from the corner of my eye at Kash's funeral, sitting tall and sharp-eyed in his pew, his full wavy mane of white hair falling gracefully back from his prominent nose. I remember thinking how beautiful he was and wondering if he'd ever realized, finally, that he was an attractive man. He called himself "a big gawky lanky son-of-a-bitch" and often said he wasn't very good looking. "Who'd want to date me?" he'd ask, half smiling and half serious, as if he were sixteen.

He couldn't sleep for thinking of her. He became feverish. He considered his sins. He thought of how miserable his state was as compared to her pure elfin loveliness. His schoolwork suffered. He played basketball like a drunken man. A dozen times he made up his mind to call her for a date. A dozen times he talked himself out of it. Once he actually climbed into the telephone booth downstairs in the hall and closed the door with his long legs jammed inside and dialed her number, 85823. He heard her phone ring, heard her lift the

receiver, heard her soft voice. But then, at the last moment,
he jerked down the hook and disconnected himself.
Wanderlust

After Kash's funeral, Dad and I looked through photos
and memorabilia in Uncle Ed's steamer trunk. Dad said he'd
been keeping the trunk since Ed's death so that he could
share the experience with me, and he stayed up past midnight to talk about Ed and his childhood. "I really miss him.
He was my first playmate. We used to play in the grass together." We both burst into tears over an old photo of the six
young Feikema brothers, standing together arm in arm, so
young and innocent. Then Dad and Tom discussed black
holes and Supreme Court Justice Clarence Thomas. ("Guilty,"
Dad said. "I believe Anita Hill.") He usually enjoyed our
times together but preferred shorter visits because he
couldn't wait to get back to his work. This time he asked us
to stay longer, and going on my gut feeling that my days with
him were numbered, I persuaded Tom and the boys to stay.

Less than a month later, in early April, Fred, Tom, the
boys, and I took Dad to see the Minnesota Twins play the
Chicago Cubs in an exhibition game at the Metrodome in
Minneapolis. There had been a teasing baseball rivalry in
our family for years, between Dad's beloved National
League Cubs and Fred's beloved American League Twins,
and finally father and son were able to watch the two teams
together. When Fred pulled Dad's car up outside our living-
room apartment window and Dad jimmied his still-giant
body out of the front seat and small-stepped toward the
front door, my heart caught. He was bent over, no longer
trying to straighten his back as he had even a few weeks before. (Once, when he was around seventy, he constructed a
shoulder brace out of old metal hangers and a few pieces of
wood that he wore daily to straighten his back. It looked like

a small cross. "I'm not going to be an old bent-over guy!" he said.)

> It is a spectacle to see the great earth dying.
>
> Slowly the drouth wrinkles the skin of the old creature. The veins, the hidden rivers and once-welling springs, dry up. The subsoil becomes brittle, and crumbles, and caves in. The topsoil crumbles, too, and collapses. And crevasses open the body.
>
> Meanwhile, the wind pounds the black skin into fine bits of gray. It bears the rich soil away, hurling and scattering it afar. Soon the deep sands and clays lie exposed.
>
> The stones and the boulders that the earth has held warmly for millions of years become traitors. They split and curve the wind into sharp, whirling, tearing eddies.
>
> *The Golden Bowl*

Dad ate a hot dog and serenely watched the Cubs beat the Twins. Then we went home, had dinner, and talked; he was as alert and intelligent as ever but slower physically than I'd ever seen him. I had a sense of him pausing in space, not climbing uphill as always, but not tumbling downhill, either. Fred mentioned a CAT scan Dad had had in late March that showed a number of pinpoint strokes at the back of his head. "Yes," Dad said, "about average for a guy my age, Doc says." He reflected on old friends who'd had similar strokes, as if he were talking about aging horses out in the barn. His face showed wonder at what was happening to his body and total acceptance of what was, at least, the doctor's truth. He stroked the back of his head with his huge hands. "It's real amazing to hear about all this," he said, "but I feel fine. My writing's just as good. In fact, it's better. To think that I've finally learned how to write at my age."

"What do you mean?" I asked.

"Keep it simple. Take out all the extraneous stuff. The pomposity. The wind."

"Do you like the writing you're doing on *Black Earth* better than your writing in *Green Earth*? *Green* is so rich, like a tree full of ripe fruit and brightly colored birds. I still think it's your best book."

His face reddened with pleasure. "Well, I thank you for saying that. And you may be right. But I like the way I'm writing now. Maybe that's why it feels better than anything I've ever written, because it's what I'm doing now and the others are all done. It's just different from *Green Earth*. There's nothing extra getting in my way. I feel like I'm holding on to the reins and the horses are pulling me straight ahead with no doubts or detours. I can't wait to get back to it."

That night he said, "I'll probably have more strokes in time, Freya."

"Do you recall feeling a little confused around Uncle Ed's funeral, Dad? Maybe you had a stroke then?"

"Maybe so," he said, "but I don't want to discuss Ed's funeral in those terms."

"Have you considered asking Fred to live with you for a few extra months before he moves into his own digs?"

"Oh, no, I'd rather be alone," he said, and grinned. "That Fred is so popular, you know. The whole town of Luverne is crazy about him. It's wonderful. But he gets too many phone calls. I've got ladies I want to call, too, you know."

I'd written and called Dad many times after he turned eighty to ask if he wanted some help at home: Meals on Wheels, a housekeeper, or someone to plow the driveway. He said Meals on Wheels was "good for people who decide to call themselves senior citizens, but not for me, and besides, I've got a garden." But Fred and his pal, Ben Vander Kooi, were able to convince Dad to hire a woman to clean house twice a month. "Now I can say good-bye to Fredericka," he said. "She's my female twin, you know, who lives here with me. Boy oh boy, I'm lucky—no more Fredericka vacuuming and scrubbing floors! Though every now and then I'll have to take her out and dust her off when Master Frederick makes a mess." As for plowing the long driveway, he did that himself until his last winter, when Vance Walgrave, his neighbor, took over the chore. I can still see Dad coming in from the subzero cold at eighty: his stiffly frozen, worn blue jeans, the old greasy gray coat frayed at the elbows and wrists and collar, the two layers of unraveling, frequently mended work gloves, the ancient brown fur hat— and under the hat his beet-red, wind-blasted face, ice clinging to the hairs in his ears, drops of moisture hanging half frozen from his nose, eyelashes crusted with snow, spark-blue eyes peering out. "Whaugh! What a wind! Took my breath for a while—but I made 'er."

In June, Tom, the kids, and I moved into our new house. When I called Dad once a week, he spoke of two events he looked forward to: his brother Henry was coming to visit, and all his old writing students at the University of South Dakota were having a reunion to celebrate their published work and to honor him as their former writing professor. When I demanded details of the rest of his life, he'd say, "I'm feeling great. *Black Earth*'s coming along beautifully. Everything's fine." But there was a notable difference in our communication. While Dad preferred letters and always responded promptly, it was common for him to answer the phone almost gruffly. "Manfred here. Oh. Freya. I can't talk. I'm watching my show on TV right now." Or, "Hi. I'm busy reading. I'll call you back some other time." Once or twice when we were both younger I was so insulted by his irritated tone of voice (he wasn't angry with me, he was angry at having his concentration disturbed) that I waited months before I called him back. But in the last year of his life he called me as often as I called him. He talked longer and was never the first to say it was time to hang up. He asked in more detail what I was doing and what Tom and the boys were up to, and he sometimes said, at the end, "I love you, Freya. Give Rowan and Bly a big hug from their Pake."

On Thursday, July 21, Fred called and asked me to come down to Luverne as soon as I could to discuss what kind of help Dad might need living alone at Roundwind. He said Dad had gone "downhill" since April and "considerably downhill" since the end of June. Several townspeople had mentioned that Dad sometimes seemed confused during conversations, and Marya had alerted Fred on Monday, July 18, that Dad should not be alone. She said she'd stay with him until Tom and I arrived. "He must be having some more pinpoint strokes," Fred said. Tom and I called Dad immediately, inviting ourselves down for a few days, and Dad said "come ahead" and "I feel fine."

We arrived at Roundwind at 7:00 P.M. Friday. Dad was sitting in his big blue armchair in his TV room, and he greeted me with a big bear hug without getting up, grinning delightedly. "There you are! Good! I've been watching TV and napping."

As soon as I sat down across from him, I noticed the right side of his mouth sagging and saw that he could not move his left hand or left foot effectively. While Dad chatted with Rowan and Bly, I said to Tom, "It looks like he's had a stroke. I wonder if he was like this when Fred called, or if he's having a stroke even as we speak." Marya was not there, and when Fred arrived moments later he pointed to Dad's hand and foot. Dad seemed to take no notice of his impairment, so I said, "Dad, your mouth is sagging on the right side and your left hand and foot aren't moving the same as your right hand and foot. Do you feel it?"

"Not really," he said. He got up then and half dragged himself toward the kitchen. Tom and I were shocked at how weak he was.

"See, Dad, your foot is dragging."

"Yeah, that's my bad knee," he said. "I'm gonna get it fixed like I did the other one."

When we pressed him, he admitted his foot and hand had been bothering him "off and on in the past few weeks." He said that he'd been to the doctor about it a week before and that his car had broken down on the way home. "Had to ask a neighbor for some help," he said. "But I'll pay him back later."

Fred said Dad had gotten a loaner, but after his second visit to the doctor, he had somehow lost control of the new car and rammed it into a number of other vehicles in the hospital parking lot.

Dad looked sheepish. "Yeah, got my damned big foot caught under the accelerator and couldn't stop her."

I called Dad's doctor at the hospital and asked the switchboard to have him call back as soon as he could. Meanwhile Dad carried on lively conversations with all of us, discussing time and space and rocket science and literature and the past and his writing and O. J. Simpson ("Not guilty. And not for the reasons you might think, Freya"). But his thinking was fuzzy when it came to actual time and his own body functions.

When I was able to get him to concentrate on how he was feeling, he told us a frightening story. I'm not sure when the event took place because at first Dad said it happened "last November," which would have been in 1993, exactly a month after I first sensed he might not live much longer. Later, when he told the story to his doctor, Dad said, "It happened in February of 1994, when Ed died." And still later, repeating the story for another doctor, he said it had "just happened" and that was why he'd gone to the doctor twice in one week in mid-July.

Whether it was November, February, or July, the story went like this: Dad was going out to the mailbox to pick up the mail at 10:30, as he always did. (His life was very structured. Certain chores were done at certain times.) On his way back, he suddenly felt "a dark terror deep in my bones, but I wasn't sure why I was so frightened. I wasn't even sure if it was coming from inside of me or from the world out there, you know?" (He made a wide sweep with his long arm to indicate the prairie outside the window.) "So I went in the house and into the kitchen to make a cup of tea to calm myself. After I put the teapot on the burner I glanced up at the calendar on the wall, and suddenly all the numbers on the calendar were falling off the pages. Flowing down the wall. I couldn't tell what day it was because there were no more days. It was the most frightened I've ever been in my life, and a terrible black feeling gripped my body, mostly in my chest. The teapot fell out of my hand, and I dropped backward against the counter until I was sitting on the floor. It was terrifying. I wished I wasn't alone." Pause. "Now what do you think that was? My God, it was terrible!"

I said, "I don't know, Dad. I wonder if it was some kind of a stroke?"

"I thought of that, but I don't think so. It was more than a stroke."

"The end of time?" Tom said.

"Yes. Exactly." He shook his head. "What an experience."

I remembered my strange premonition or "vision" nine months earlier: the sudden knowledge as I walked toward the house at Roundwind that my father might not live much longer. Not long afterward Dad had deeply felt the "end of time," the presence of death, as he walked through the same backyard.

> *March 1, 1981*
> I'm having a grave time preparing for my "presidential lecture" on March 30th. Mostly because I'm venturing into another field. But I think I'm right. And it doesn't hurt to ask questions. I'm shaping the whole thing in the form of a question. I learned from that book I bought when Freya took me to her sauna lady (*The Dancing Wu Li Masters* by Gary Zukav) that quantum mechanics has suggested that there is something going on that is faster than the speed of light, and that right away suggests to me that there is no time. They say all is one instantaneously at any given moment: past, present and future—so, if true, where is time then?

When Dr. Vogel called (covering for Dad's favorite, Dr. Kuiper), I described Dad's symptoms carefully. He said Dad was "most likely" having a series of strokes. He mentioned "all those pinpoint strokes" from the CAT scan in March and said we should not be surprised if Dad continued to have stroke after stroke over the next day or so because "when they start coming along like this, they usually continue."

"Should we bring him to the hospital?"

"Not necessarily. If he's comfortable, no use bringing him in unless he wants to come. There's no way we can stop strokes in the hospital, anyway. And if he has a massive stroke, which is quite possible, he'll die at home, something I know he'd prefer."

"You're right about that," I said.

"But bring him in on Monday if you like," he said.

I hung up and went back into the living room to look at my father. When I heard the doctor say that Dad might be dying of a series of strokes, that he might even die that day, I was so shocked I didn't feel the impact of the words until weeks later.

The next morning Dad was worse. He dropped his first cup of coffee on the floor, breaking the mug, and then dropped a second mug because he couldn't remember to use his right hand. "What a damn clumsy guy I am," he said.

"You're not clumsy, Dad. Your hand isn't working properly."

"Oh, it'll be fine," he said. "I'm just tired."

When Uncle Henry called, Dad spoke to him as if he were doing perfectly. He wanted to appear strong and in charge, even with his closest brother. But after the call he said, "I'm tired. I'm going back to bed. I'm glad you and Tom are here because now I know I need some help." He added that he planned to read from *Black Earth* for the Carnegie reading series at Blue Mound that evening. He leaned almost his full weight against Tom, dragging his foot behind him as he staggered slowly to bed. "God, Tom, you're a bull of a man!" Tom tucked Dad into bed and came out into the living room and said he didn't see how Dad was going to make it through his speech. I called Dr. Vogel again, and he said to let Dad do anything he cared to do or *could* do, so Tom and Fred went to town to get Dad a walker—Dad weighed 240 pounds, and Tom knew he couldn't support him all the way from the car to his chair for the reading.

Dad made his speech. He had essentially no use of his left arm or leg, and Rowan, Bly, Tom, and Fred had to pull him out of the backseat of the car and get him onto his walker. Then Tom and the walker got him to his chair. Fred, strongly aware that this might be our father's last speech, gave a very moving introduction, after which Dad read from *Black Earth* and answered questions. He was humorously entertaining and perfectly intelligible, and he sat and signed books afterward. One of his best young gal pals, the poet Barbara Baker, sat on his lap for a while, and he was cheery as hell. When he got home, he asked for pie and ice cream and went straight to sleep, satisfied and exhilarated and exhausted.

By Sunday morning he had lost the concept of what hour, day, or month it was, but he got out of bed to sit at the breakfast table when we told him what time it was. "I always sit at my table first and have a morning cup of coffee, Freya. You know that." I had to hold his cup for him. Then he insisted that Tom help him to his blue chair in front of the TV. His breathing was beginning to sound labored, but when Dr. Kuiper called he said it was OK to keep him home till Monday if we stayed with him all the time. That day Dad dozed, watched TV, and chatted with the kids about baseball. Mom drove over from Sioux Falls with a Chinese dinner for everyone, "but especially for Tom because he is such a big help to all of us." Mom and Tom got into a political discussion, and the kids played basketball outside with Fred while Marya and I chatted. It was the first time in years that I'd had dinner with everyone in our family at the same time, but it felt almost meaningless to me whenever I looked at my father's mottled, puffy face and faraway eyes. He ate two platefuls of food and two desserts, and then Tom and the boys supported him while he staggered to his bed.

After he was asleep, Fred and Tom and I had the first of many discussions about Dad. Everyone, including the Luverne doctors, assumed he was having a series of strokes. But how disabled would he be after the strokes? Would they kill him? If he lived, where should he spend his time? In a nursing home? Or in his own home with full- or part-time care? I hated the discussion because we were all worn out from fright and shock and sadness.

After Fred left, Dad awakened and wanted to go to the bathroom. This was no small task, although the bathroom was only twenty feet from his bed. In just a few hours Dad had lost even more control of his left side, and he found the walker too unwieldy, even with our help. His giant body slowly sank to the floor until he was on his knees, and then he crumpled slowly to one side, where he lay staring up at us with wild, surprised eyes. Tom crouched and lifted him, taking almost all of Dad's dead weight and tearing the tendon in his elbow in the process. Somehow the two of them staggered to the bathroom with Dad, between gasps, exhorting, "Good, Tom, that's a boy. I knew you could do it. What a man you are, Tom. My God, what a man." When they staggered back ten minutes later, Dad looked relieved and exhausted, and Tom was white-faced. Somehow he managed to help Dad pivot and sink into the bed. "A bull of a man," Dad muttered again and fell asleep.

Tom went to bed and I sat and watched Dad. His harsh breathing terrified me. I worried that he would die that night. In time, tiring, I crept into bed with Tom.

"I hope Dad either dies or gets well enough to write again—no middle ground. I hope that's not a mean thing to say."

"Not at all," Tom said. "You can be sure your dad hopes the same thing."

During the night Dad woke us twice because he turned on his radio, saying he wanted "some news of the world" and "some company." It was almost like dealing with a two-year-old: Dad didn't know or care if it was the middle of the night and could not understand why we didn't want to stay up and chat. Finally, Tom was able to convince him that we needed a few hours of sleep, no matter what time it was, and he kept his radio off until dawn.

On Monday Dad had even more difficulty breathing. He was lying on his bed after breakfast, snoring deeply, and I lay down beside him. I felt he was very near death, that if we didn't take him to the hospital he'd be dead in a few hours, a day at most. I considered, as fully as I could, whether to let him lie there and die in his own bed in the beautiful rock house he loved. He'd hauled thousands of fieldstones in the trunk of his old car to build the place. I could hear the prairie grass whispering just outside the open bedroom window. If Tom and I drove Dad into town and signed him into the hospital "system," his doctors would try to stretch out his life for a few days or weeks because that was their job, and then he'd die anyway. He might even end up in a nursing home or a home for the elderly, which he always said he would hate. ("Freya, I'll kill myself first, like Hemingway. I'll blow my head off. I've been to rest homes to visit. I have nothing in common with those people. I have a young man's brain.") If I called the hospital now, the last chance Dad might have for a quick and basically painless and peaceful death at home might be gone. He was going and he was going fast. Why not let him go now?

But then I reasoned, "What if he can get better? What if he comes out of this and can walk outdoors, or visit with friends and family, or even write again? Who am I to let him die now?" But all the time I had a gut feeling he was not going to get better. So time passed (time as I knew it because he was now beyond time), and I contemplated. I liked lying there next to him. I felt it would be a good way to die, lying in your own bed next to a daughter who loved you. The only better thing might be to die outside, lying in the longhaired grass with the sun on your face. Finally, I turned to the phone and lifted the receiver to call the hospital. This was not my life, not my choice. I only hoped my father would not have to pay for my decision with days and months of pain and hospitalization. I imitated Dad's breathing over the phone for Dr. Kuiper, and he said to get him to the hospital sooner rather than later. Tom drove our car down the steep hill on the west side of the house so that Dad wouldn't have to climb his front stairs, and we somehow managed to get him into the car.

At Luverne Community Hospital Dad was given oxygen. Within half an hour his breathing sounded normal again, and he became livelier and more cheerful than he'd been at home. He knew the answer to every question they asked except the time of day.

Dr. Kuiper took Fred, Tom, and me into the hall where he said that Dad would stabilize in a few days and that we should look into a nursing home or full-time care at home. Fred said the Mary Jane Brown Good Samaritan Center was full, so Dr. Kuiper agreed to put Dad into a hospital "swing bed," a status that would permit him to eventually go home if he got better. We told Dr. Kuiper of Dad's living will, and he read over a copy of it with us. The will specified that if Dad were incapacitated, Fred was primarily responsible for his finances, and I was primarily responsible for decisions about his health care. Dad wanted to be allowed to die naturally rather than exist in a vegetative state on a respirator.

> *January 19, 1990*
> Freya, please file this away with your private papers. Okay?
> Dad
> TO WHOM IT MAY CONCERN
> Should I ever have an accident, or have a stroke, or have any other calamity hit me which should render me helpless or brain dead or make me seem no more than a vegetable, I hereby request that I not be hooked to a life-support system

to "keep me alive." Please let me go. I wish for the deons*
that make up my body to join with their brother deons in
the Great Outspread of the Universe.
Written this day, January 18, 1990, by
Frederick Feikema Manfred, Sr.

That evening Tom and I asked Dr. Kuiper if it was OK to
leave Dad and go home for a few days before we came back
for a longer stay to help get him situated. Dr. Kuiper said it
was perfectly safe to do so. Dad was talking zestfully, reading letters, and watching TV. For dinner he'd eaten a stack of
blueberry pancakes that Fred whipped up in his apartment
across the street from the hospital, plus a hospital dinner,
plus a gigantic banana split Rowan and Bly bought for him.
Every thirty minutes he teased the nurse who came in to ask
him the usual litany of questions:

"Who's the president, Mr. Manfred?"

"I don't care as long as it's not Ronald Reagan."

" OK. And do you know where you are?"

"In a clean white room with a clean white beautiful
nurse."

"Now, Mr. Manfred."

"Luverne Hospital, intensive care. But say, you better get
me some ice cream before you ask me any more questions."

"Mr. Manfred, I already got you some ice cream. Don't
you remember?"

"I know you did, but I'd sure like some more."

Just three weeks earlier, on June 30, Dad had stopped

* *Deon* was Dad's word for a subatomic force, which he described in a
footnote to the poem "Seventy" (*Winter Count II*): "The final bit of in-
destructible matter, the basic building block of the universe, which I
predict physicists will soon find, and discover that it is neither particle
nor wave, but something alive."

working on *Black Earth*, the novel he'd begun in April 1993. Now, when I told him I had to go home for a few days, he took my hand in his bigger hand and asked me to be sure the novel was "safe" because he wasn't sure where he'd put it after his reading at Blue Mound: "I don't want anything to happen to it, because I'm going to finish it just as soon as I'm through here," he said. "Please locate it for me."

I drove to Roundwind and found the unbound manuscript on the floor next to Dad's bed in its ancient fake-suede "briefcase." I gathered the briefcase into my arms as if I'd found a baby bird under a tree without a mother bird to watch over it. The manuscript seemed so vulnerable and precious to me, lying all by itself on the floor in the house that was now empty of my father's presence. When we stopped back at the hospital to say good-bye, I showed it to Dad and said I'd take care of it. "I'd like to read it," I said.

He grinned. "Great! You can give me your impressions before I finish the last part, which is about what happened to all six of us brothers after our father died."

While Tom drove us home, I looked through the manuscript and saw that Dad had begun each day's work with an entry in the margin, giving the date and a daily comment, usually about the weather. He'd begun writing fifteen months earlier, working steadily with no break for ten months, three pages a day, one to two pages if he felt tired. His "weather reports" were charmingly short: "Cool," "Warming Up," "Sunny," "Rain," "Beautiful Lilacs!" "Clear Blue Skies," "Tornadoes Last Night," "Stegner Died Yesterday," "Muggy," "Sticky," "Dark and Gloomy," "Clouds Have Fallen to Earth," "Audrey Arner and Friend Dropped By," "Sprinkles," "Chilly; It Hurts," "White Frost, Cool Sun," and in late October 1993, "Stiff from falling on the floor at Henry's," "Tired from the last weekend," and "Lethargic." In November it was "Freddy Nearby" and "Sunny," and then, on

January 31, 1994, he wrote "Doldrums" and stopped working for six weeks except for February 11 and 14 (a three-page day), when he wrote, "Couldn't sleep last night."

Within days Dad's brother Edward Feikema died. Ed's death, plus a series of colds and flus accompanied by frequently prescribed antibiotics, and the death of Kash Vander Kooi in March, slowed Dad's progress. In March he wrote only on the sixteenth, seventeenth, eighteenth, and twenty-second. But on April 4 he began to write again every other day, and then every day until the middle of May, although he no longer jotted down his weather report at the beginning of each day's work. In the last third of May he wrote only on the nineteenth (two lines) and the twenty-third (one and a half pages). Then he skipped to June 7 (one page), June 8 (three pages), and went on every day again until June 20 (two pages). On June 23, he wrote on the side of page 408: "Muggy. Had to fix my armchair up here" (the old armchair in the "tepee," his writing studio). On June 24, 27, 28, and 29, he wrote one page a day and finished the last two pages of *Black Earth* on June 30 with a paragraph in which Free (Dad as a younger man) and Sherman (Uncle Henry as a young man) watch their father's coffin being lowered into the ground:

> Their loud grief, their tears, made Free and Sherman realize they had never let their father know how much they loved him and respected him, how much they owed him for his example of the grave dignity of the fully mature male. They had yet to learn how to become the beloved patriarchs for their own children, Pa's grandchildren.
>
> *Black Earth*

Those were the last words Dad wrote.

John Calvin Rezmerski, who interviewed Dad extensively a year before he died, said Dad also told him that *Black*

Earth was to be longer, telling the story not only of the six sons but also of their families after their "beloved patriarch" died. I would have enjoyed seeing myself, my siblings, and my cousins described as youngsters, but that was not to be. Dad was too tired to write from his hospital bed, although he spoke every day of getting up to Roundwind to "finish *Black Earth*." Marilyn Forrest, a dear friend who had flown in from Alaska to watch over Dad in the hospital for several weeks, told me that his fingers were typing on imaginary typewriter keys as he dozed.

I edited *Black Earth* the year after Dad died and found that the book has a strong dramatic arc and a powerful ending. It's possible that if Dad had known he had only a few months to live, he might have chosen to revise what he had, rather than adding more chapters. Dad always cut at least two lines from every page before he sent the book to a publisher. "No matter how good a writer you are, there's no page that can't lose two lines." But, miraculously, the novel ends conclusively, with Dad's father's coffin being lowered into the ground.

As soon as we got home, we lit a fire in our fireplace—it was a curiously cold July night. I sat and stared into the flames while Tom worked on his writing and Rowan and Bly threw a baseball back and forth in the backyard.

Twenty-four hours later Fred called to say that Dad was being rushed by ambulance to McKennan Hospital in Sioux Falls. A new CAT scan had revealed that Dad's problems were caused not by a series of strokes but rather by a rapidly growing tumor that had pushed his brain "out of its axis." The brain was so swollen and the tumor took up so much space, Dr. Kuiper said, that "any other man, with a smaller cranium, would have been dead a week ago. The fact that he has motor activity is astonishing because there should be no movement at all."

"Why didn't the tumor show up on the CAT scan he had three months ago?" I asked Fred.

"If it was there, no one saw it," Fred said. "He's in such bad shape he could die on the way to Sioux Falls, so I have to hang up now and follow the ambulance in my car. I'll call you as soon as I can."

> "Whaugh!" A great belly grunt burped up from the white sands directly in front of him. And with a tremendous tumbler's heave of body, a silvertipped gray she-grizzly, *Ursus horribilis*, rose up before him on two legs. "Whaugh!" Two little brown grizzly cubs ducked cowering and whimpering behind the old lady. . . .
>
> Hugh backed in terror, his heart suddenly burning hot and bounding around in his chest. The little arteries down his big Scotch nose wriggled red. His breath caught. The sense of things suddenly unraveling, of the end coming on, of being no longer in control of either things or his life, possessed him.
>
> She was as big as a great bull standing on two legs. She was so huge on her two legs that her incredible speed coming toward him actually seemed slow. Time stiffened, poured like cold molasses.
>
> She roared. She straddled toward him on her two rear legs. She loomed over him, silver neck ruffed and humped, silver head pointed down at him. Her pink dugs stuck out at him. She stunk of dogmusk.
>
> She hung over him, huge furry arms ready to cuff and strike. Her red-stained ivorygray claws, each a lickfinger long, each curved a little like a cripple's iron hook, closed and unclosed.
>
> Hugh's eyes set; stiffened; yet he saw it all clearly. Time passed slow—yet was fast.
>
> *Lord Grizzly*

Fred called a few hours later from Sioux Falls. Doctors were giving Dad steroids and a diuretic called mannitol to reduce the swelling of the brain, but he could die that night if the drugs didn't work, and they often didn't. Fred asked if Dad could be put on a respirator for a short time as a second measure to save his life if the drugs failed. I reread his living will, which said respirators were OK if they were short term and necessary to save his life, and said yes.

By the time we arrived at the hospital's intensive care unit the next morning, Dad was "out of serious danger" and joking with doctors, although he told me his ambulance driver the night before had resembled Charon, the man who rows the spirits of the dead across the River Styx.

An internist stopped by to tell Dad that they had to do a biopsy to see if his brain tumor was malignant. I didn't like the way the internist seemed annoyed every time we asked a question and didn't look anyone in the eye when he answered. Luckily, Dr. Freeman, a neurologist who had once attended my mother, also stopped by. Warmly, kindly, expressing the utmost concern for Dad, he told us the tumor was large, fast growing, and "not a good thing." He said he'd once taken a creative writing class from Dad. "I care about him as a man and as a literary figure. He is a tremendously giving teacher as well as a great writer." Dr. Freeman said he'd talk with us more after the biopsy results, but ten minutes later he returned to us with a worried face. He'd been looking at Dad's CAT scan again, and he shared with us that his mother had died of a similar type of brain cancer and that it was probably malignant and would soon lead to death.

We stayed at Mom's apartment, our sons entertained by the pool, the TV, and the nearby Empire Mall. The adults were in chaos. Was the tumor malignant? Would it be treatable if it were malignant? If it were treatable, would Dad have radiation or chemotherapy or both? Who would take care of him, and where would he live while undergoing treatment?

Dad was moved out of intensive care while we waited for the biopsy. Over the next few days many of his favorite pals came by to chat with him: Gordy Gits, English teacher and Luverne mayor; Wayne S. Knutson, Distinguished Professor Emeritus of English from the University of South Dakota; Art Huseboe, director of the Center for Western Studies at Augustana, and many others. Although he hated being in the hospital, Dad truly enjoyed talking with his friends, and when they weren't around, he engaged each doctor and nurse he met in conversation or challenging discussion.

One of Dad's most interesting encounters occurred an hour before he was scheduled to have several holes drilled in his skull for the biopsy. A woman wearing a brightly flowered dress with a white lace collar and carrying a small white Bible stopped in a room down the hall. A few moments later she started toward Dad's room, and I quickly asked a nurse, "Who's that?"

"One of our chaplains, making a call."

"On whom?"

"On your dad, most likely. Before every operation, however minor, a hospital chaplain is assigned to visit the patient in case he or she wishes spiritual guidance. It's just routine."

"She's in for more than routine if she visits Dad," I said. And I pulled up a chair to watch the unfolding drama.

The chaplain was pretty, with a hint of red in her curly hair and a sweet, almost innocent face sprinkled with light freckles. She introduced herself to Dad by name. He nodded.

"What do you do?" he asked.

"I'm the hospital chaplain."

"And what do you want with me?"

"My job is to visit with all the patients who are about to have an operation."

"For what purpose?"

"Well, I guess it's to see where they stand spiritually. To see if they'd like to talk or pray for a while before their operation."

"Ah. May I ask, what religion are you?"

"Me?"

"Yes. I was wondering how you were raised?"

"Actually, I'm a Catholic by upbringing."

"Catholic. That's a strong religion. A lot of beautiful words and phrases in the Catholic religion. Some surprising works of art, too. The Catholic church has an amazing history. Have you read much about it?"

She fiddled with her lace collar a moment. "No, I really don't know much about Catholic history."

"Well, it's an unforgettable story—the Catholic church. I'll tell you a few things you might want to look into." And Dad proceeded to describe the history of Catholicism, paying special note to Catholic art and Catholic writings from every century to the present. Woven into his comments were a few remarks about some of the helpful or beautiful things the Catholic church had given to mankind and a few other remarks about some of the less helpful and uglier aspects of the church. All very kindly said, of course.

The lovely chaplain's mouth fell slightly open during Dad's long discourse. Finally he finished and waved one hand. "That's a start," he said.

"Well, well," she said. "I guess I should have studied more about it."

"Yes, it's very interesting stuff."

"But Mr. Manfred, the reason I came here today was to see how you are doing spiritually during this time of great stress."

"Well, tell me," he answered, "what are you going to do with that information once I supply it?"

"That depends on where you are spiritually at this time. Perhaps I could guide you along the way."

Dad laid his great head back on the pillow a moment. He closed his eyes briefly. "Well, tell me, as chaplain here, have you read much philosophy? Philosophical writings?"

A touch of nervousness again. "No. No, I haven't."

"Then you might try it sometime. I have a list of good ones for you. Try Nietzsche and Schopenhauer and Wittgenstein and Plato. Those are wonderful guys, wonderful minds. Give them a try."

"But . . . Mr. Manfred—"

"And another thing," he interrupted. "What about poetry? Who are your favorite poets? Or writers? In your role as chaplain do you refer people at all to literature?"

"Well, I don't read literature really—certainly I never read poetry. But maybe I should try some."

"Oh, yes! It will be well worth your time. Those guys will take you somewhere. Try Chaucer and Whitman, and don't forget Emily Dickinson. She's my favorite."

The chaplain's mouth was open much of the time now. She stroked her white Bible with one hand. "But, Mr. Manfred, I came here to find out what your relationship with God might be."

"My background was Christian Reformed," he said. "And as you know, they make some pretty strong statements."

"Yes, I know," she said.

"Pretty strong stuff. Some of it too strong." Dad's eyes lit up suddenly. "Say, you wouldn't have one of those Christian Reformed guys right here would you?"

"You mean a minister?"

"No, just anyone who's raised Christian Reformed. Someone who's sick here in the hospital like me. Aren't any of your patients Christian Reformed?"

"Why, no—I've not run across that today."

"Well, it's too bad," Dad said. "But if you find one later to-day, could you rustle him up for me?"

"Rustle him up?"

"I'd like you to bring him around here so I can talk with him. I like to argue with those guys—it perks them up. If you can find me someone, send him over, and we'll talk. It'll do him some good, and me, too!"

She smiled now. "Well, of course, I'll keep that in mind. But Mr. Manfred, can we spend one moment on your personal relationship with God?"

"Well, I'll tell you. When it comes to a personal creed I think I most take after my Grandpa. He was not an atheist—he was an agnostic, and he said the best thing about religion that I have ever heard."

"I see," she said warily.

"Yes. In fact, Grandpa made the one statement about religion that I could wholeheartedly agree with."

"And what . . . what was that, Mr. Manfred?"

"Grandpa used to say—and it's the truest thing I've ever heard. He said this: 'God is in you—and he is smiling.'"

The chaplain repeated the first part of what Dad had said. "God is in you . . . ?"

"That's right. 'God is in you—and he is smiling.'"

The chaplain slid to her feet. "Well, Mr. Manfred, I can see you're doing just fine."

"Yes, I am," he said.

And she departed, her Bible held to her breast with both hands.

"Nice to meet you, lady!" he called to her.

But she was halfway down the hall and must not have heard, for she did not reply.

· · ·

The day after the biopsy we met Dad's smiling, vigorous, al-most prancing biopsy surgeon, who said even though the cancer (a small-cleaved lymphocytic lymphoma) was malig-nant, it was "the good kind of cancer," not the "bad kind of cancer," because it was "treatable." "Bad" cancers could not be treated with radiation, he said, and we took this to mean that the cancer was curable. "Great!" Dad said.

We also met Dr. Nordstrom, the radiologist, who told me his wife had enjoyed reading some of Dad's books. He sug-gested we go to the Mayo Clinic in Rochester, Minnesota, for a second opinion because the cancer Dad had was rare, and there were only a few doctors in the country who had much experience with it. He called Dr. O'Neill and Dr. Shaw at Mayo to set up appointments.

That evening we met another doctor, Dad's oncologist, who sat in the armchair across from Dad's bed with his arms crossed over his chest and studied Dad with the sharp-eyed look of a curious but objective scientist, though he couldn't help but break into a smile now and then when Dad came up with a funny story or an interchange with the nurses.

I didn't care for the oncologist. He barely shook my hand, avoided my eyes, and answered my questions in a mildly condescending tone of voice. ("He's not user friendly," Tom said later.) When we asked for in-depth information about Dad's chances for survival, he said no one had any idea what would happen because there were not enough statistical case studies of Dad's kind of cancer to know the chances of success or failure. "He could die today, or tomorrow, like the rest of us. He might even live for another five years." Perhaps the oncologist didn't wish to tell us what he knew from the few available statistics, or perhaps he didn't have the statis-tics—either way, he didn't improve my opinion of him. If he knew of doctors who had the statistics, however small, he ought to have told us how to reach them. Or, if he knew the statistics were frightening, he should have told us about them anyway because we made it very clear we wanted to know, good news or bad. One day to five years is a very large window of time for an exhausted, frightened, worried family to consider, especially since Dad had so little money for home care or rest homes, if those were necessary, and most especially since we knew Dad would not want to be alive if he could not finish writing *Black Earth.*

No matter what any doctor said about the tumor, even when they called it malignant, Dad always referred to it as "an encroachment" or "a small growth." When friends and relatives asked why he was hospitalized, he said he had a bad knee and needed an operation. I couldn't tell if his sometimes clouded mind had settled on the knee and lost track of the rest of the information, whether he knew exactly what was wrong but didn't care to share it, or whether he was mulling over events and possibilities and arriving at a truth he could live with for the time being. Uncle Henry, who had lived with cancer for years, said Dad should "accept the cancer or he'd never learn to live with it." And he added, "After talking with Fred, I'm wondering if his doctors have been straight and up-front with him."

"They've been straight about what the cancer is called and about the fact that it's malignant," I told him, "but I don't think they are being very clear about his chances for survival or what his life might be like for the next few months and years."

"Maybe I'll try and talk with them," Uncle Henry said.

"I'll try again, too," I said.

Meanwhile, I waited for my father to verbalize what was happening to him. He was usually disarmingly honest, with both feet solidly on the ground, although sometimes he'd present the truth *rewritten*, the way he wanted to believe it, to gain the courage to get through a disastrous situation.

But I was always able to connect with him about what was real when I had to. For example, when both my sister and brother were simultaneously experiencing terrifying life crises, Dad kept insisting that everything was "going to be fine," would eternally be "fine," and that he was "doing very well" in dealing with his feelings about the crises. But when I expressed my own fears and hopes for Fred and Marya, he immediately admitted his own and started to cry. He never lied to me, or to himself in front of me, about anything important. When he continued to avoid referring to his tumor as cancerous, I decided it didn't matter. It was his body. Whether his brain was too befogged or he was adjusting to what was happening to him in his own fashion, he probably knew instinctively what kind of attitude would yield the most positive result.

> When he was a boy of seven he had sometimes run crying to his father's bed after a bad dream. "Father, let me lie under your folded robe." And always his father had taken him in his arms and held him until morning. His father was always warm, his arms always strong. His father smelled of a windy day on a high dusty hill. This was because his father was one of those who worshiped the Thunders and often sat on a high place waiting for them to come.
>
> *Conquering Horse*

Tom and I went home for a week and had the flu. While I spent my days making a series of calls to McKennan Hospital, Luverne Community Hospital, and the Mayo Clinic to gain more information about brain cancer, nursing homes, and home care, Fred worked tirelessly from McKennan, trying to find the best place for Dad to stay while he underwent the required six weeks of radiation. Fred and I felt a growing pressure because McKennan was preparing to dismiss Dad. The only statement that gave me peace during these few days was something Fred said one evening: "I have faith the situation will work out for the best with collaboration. We will get Dad through to an acceptable life and death."

But my brother and I didn't agree on where Dad should stay during radiation; Tom, Mom, and Marya stayed out of the decision. Fred, backed by sound advice from McKennan Hospital discharge personnel, felt Dad should stay at a nursing home in Sioux Falls during the radiation because he'd have better physical therapy and care. Radiation side effects might be powerful, and he was already unsteady on his feet; it would be more convenient to avoid the sixty-mile roundtrip each day from Luverne. Besides, Fred added, Dad said "fine" when the Sioux Falls nursing home was mentioned to him. After radiation, Dad could move into the "swing bed" in Luverne to rest. Still later, if he were strong enough, he could go home.

But I was operating on the visual picture I had when I imagined Dad in a strange nursing home in Sioux Falls. And, when I asked Dad what he preferred, he said he wanted to go back to Luverne, even if he had to be in the hospital, because it was where he "belonged." When I presented both sides of the problem to Dr. Nordstrom, he said, "Don't tell me whether you want your Dad in Luverne or whether your brother does—just let me make my point. I have a very worried and uneasy feeling about this man in a nursing home in Sioux Falls because he has lived a life in Luverne where he is special to family, friends, and fans. Radiation patients do better at home or near home. I've seen too many sad old people in nursing homes."

When I told Dr. Nordstrom my brother's level-headed objections to Luverne, he answered, "You must first be clear on what's emotionally best for your father. Second, don't worry too much about radiation side effects. Third, the therapy and care in Luverne will be good enough. And lastly, yes, it's a big drive, but he can do it. It's the loss of home base that's the worst."

I told Fred what Dr. Nordstrom had said, but I could tell he was still not happy about Dad going back to Luverne. I asked him if he were upset because he might have to take on too much responsibility if Dad were in Luverne, and he said yes: Dad's hospital room would be right across the street from his apartment; besides, Marya might not be able to help, and Tom and I would be three and a half hours away in Minneapolis. So, with a serious illness of his own to contend with, Fred might be "on call" too often.

I said Dad would have so many friends stopping by in Luverne that Fred needn't visit every day, and if he did visit, he needn't stay for long. I promised I'd drive down every week so that Fred could rest. (We later realized that we lived at Dad's house in Luverne for thirty of the last forty-two days of his life.) I added that Dad might not make it through six weeks of radiation, and I could not bear to watch him die in Sioux Falls. So, Fred agreed, and when Tom and I were home sick, Fred and Marilyn Forrest, Dad's friend from Alaska, brought Dad back to the Luverne hospital after one week at McKennan and one radiation treatment.

Fred brought Dad's mail and paper to him every morning, checked with the doctors, and continued his innumerable tasks as manager of Dad's affairs. Marilyn also turned out to be the most thoughtful of friends; for most of ten days she sat on a chair outside Dad's room, emptying his urine bag, giving him treats, and shooing people away if he was napping. She also drove him to radiation and stopped at the Luverne Dairy Queen afterward for Dad's favorite ice cream. Then she drove back to the hospital via Roundwind so that he could sit in the car with the windows open and look out over his hillside, which was turning amber in the August heat. (He was too heavy for anyone to get him in and out of the house in a wheelchair, partly because Roundwind has a long steep staircase entrance, and approaching the sliding glass doors on the lower level requires a tricky, bumpy forty-five-degree drive over the brow of the hill.) I was also thankful for Marilyn's presence because her high degree of emotionality matched my own, and she wasn't critical of my occasional outbursts of feeling. Plus, with the utmost discretion and love, she left Tom and me alone when we wanted to visit with Dad.

> He looked up. He heard the night moaning in the leaves above. Some of the leaves were tipped with moon's gold. A few cloud lumps far above were edged with yellow-silver. If there were only a friend. Only. A friend would salve his bleeding fingers, would reassure his hoping mind. A friend would try to show him that suffering was not singular, that it helped build all lives—truths which he had trouble bringing himself to believe alone.
>
> *The Chokecherry Tree*

A few days after Dad moved back to Luverne, Fred, Tom, and I drove him to the Mayo Clinic. On the way there, Fred and Dad lay stretched out side by side in the back of our station wagon because Dad was so tired he couldn't sit up very long. Fred chatted with us while Dad dozed. When we pulled into a rest stop, Fred drained Dad's urine bag, and we hurried on. (Dad had needed a catheter off and on since his first night in the hospital because there were some days when he could not control his bladder.) Dad later told the Luverne nurses it was the "nicest trip" he'd had in a long time: "I had a lot of fun because I was with my family."

When we arrived at the impressive complex of buildings in Rochester, Fred checked in while Tom and I wheeled Dad to Dr. O'Neill's floor. While we waited in the gigantic lobby outside the doctor's office, Dad's urine bag overflowed, and

Fred had to remove Dad's trousers and wash them out in a nearby bathroom. Once we were called into Dr. O'Neill's office, Fred waved the light cotton trousers around to dry them, and we all talked. Dad, excited by the chance to see the man who was probably the world's expert on the type of cancer we were dealing with, the man who might finally tell him his prognosis, talked the most; consequently, by the time the doctor arrived at least an hour later, he was exhausted and half asleep.

After questioning Dad about whether there was lupus in his family, or any other immunosuppressant disease, and about how and when two of his five brothers had died, Dr. O'Neill asked Dad what he thought was wrong with him.

"An encroachment, a small growth," Dad answered.

"Now, Mr. Manfred," Dr. O'Neill said, "why would a man as brilliant and intelligent as you obviously are, a man who has written all those great books, be willing to allow some strange doctors from Sioux Falls to give you six weeks of dangerous and intensive radiation if the only thing you have wrong with you is a small growth or 'encroachment'?"

Dad smiled faintly. "Well, of course I wouldn't let them touch me unless it was very serious."

Having acknowledged that his situation was dangerous, Dad promptly fell asleep, snoring from time to time, and then waking again, so I was never sure how much he heard of the rest of Dr. O'Neill's remarks. The doctor explained to us that sleeping and exhaustion were major side effects of this type of cancer, and radiation would temporarily worsen the situation, forcing Dad to sleep more and more. He said that eighty percent of small-cleaved lymphatic lymphomas could be "considerably reduced" but that there were "lousy statistics" for getting this type of cancer to stay away forever. For a few months after radiation, there was "a good chance" Dad would "go back to being the way he was about a year ago, whatever state he was in then, including the ability to write novels and tell time," until the cancer returned. Fifty percent of patients relapse in eleven months, and since Dad was past eighty and already suffering from a great deal of immobility, Dr. O'Neill suspected that in six to eleven months the cancer would "certainly return, with a vengeance." Once the cancer returned, Dad might live two to six more weeks, probably in a coma at the end, but he would die a painless death.

We left Dr. O'Neill in good spirits because he wasn't vague or secretive about how long Dad might live and what he might be able to accomplish while alive. I no longer pictured Dad lying in a nursing home for months or years— maybe even the five years the oncologist had cruelly mentioned—unable to write or talk. As we left Dr. O'Neill's office, Dad said, "That's a great doc. I like him. He was direct and clear and at the same time compassionate. I'm glad we came to the Mayo Clinic. Now let's eat."

As we steered Dad through the Mayo's labyrinthic tunnels toward an underground lunchroom, I was struck by how helpful it was to have the Three Musketeers accompanying Dad. Tom was the strongman who pushed the wheelchair and asked the sharp questions he always asked. Fred was the scout and medical expert, walking ahead to find the right desk and the right room, and because of his background and experience with doctors and hospitals, his questions were always valuable. And I turned my attention to Dad's reactions and feelings, with questions concerning his well-being neither Tom nor Fred might have asked.

After lunch, our next appointment was with the head radiologist, Dr. Shaw, whose office was in a series of wood-paneled suites that resembled a sumptuous law office. We didn't have to sit in the large waiting room because a nurse ushered us immediately to Dr. Shaw's suite, where Dad fell asleep on the long, handsome couch. I found Tom some aspirin for his headache, and he lay on the floor next to Dad with the lights turned out. I sat on the floor in the richly carpeted hall and closed my eyes. Fred went off to explore. Dad woke a few times, a little lost and mixed up, but Tom reassured him, and he went back to sleep.

Dr. Shaw was very late. After we had waited more than an hour, his assistant came and talked with us for thirty minutes, but the doctor didn't appear for another half hour. We were about to leave, thinking we knew enough about the cancer from Dr. O'Neill, when Dr. Shaw arrived, apologizing profusely. He listened, smiling and nodding, to Dad's story about knocking out Joe Louis's sparring partner some fifty-five years earlier and then asked if we'd like to see slides of the four cancerous lesions from the CAT scan. Until now, no one had offered to let us see them or discussed them in such detail. The lesions looked like four black marbles, arranged like a four-leaf clover in Dad's brain. Dr. Shaw said that radiation would get rid of the lesions, and he asked Dad what he most wanted to have happen as a result of radiation.

"I want my clarity back," Dad said. "I need a clear head for long enough to finish the book."

"How long is that?"

"Six months would do it," Dad replied.

Dr. Shaw left to consult with Dr. O'Neill on the phone. When he returned, he said Dad would "probably buy time to write again with radiation." Also, after radiation, he'd be able to use his left hand and foot normally and think clearly, but he still might have some slight confusion about time. The tumor had also affected the area of the brain that controlled the bladder, which could be the reason why Dad was sometimes incontinent; but the bladder, too, would "improve with radiation."

As Tom and I pushed Dad toward the car, Fred lingered to

talk to Dr. Shaw about his recent kidney transplant and to ask if he was more likely to get the type of cancer Dad had because he was at risk for all illnesses. When he didn't come out, I walked back to look for him while Tom stayed with Dad.

"Come on, Fred, let's go."

"Coming." They shook hands. "Good-bye, Dr. Shaw."

The doctor hesitated. "One more thing," he said. "I like your dad—he's a great old guy and a brilliant artist, and I can see how much his family cares about him. I think it's best that you know . . . your dad will be very lucky to live six months."

I asked, "So he's not likely to make it for eleven months, which Dr. O'Neill said might be possible?"

"No. Dr. O'Neill and I talked again, and after six weeks of radiation your dad will have maybe three months to write on his book before the cancer returns. When it returns, there will be no pain, but your dad will be confused or in a coma and bed bound. He might lose his body functions if the cancer spreads to his lower brain before death comes. He'll need round-the-clock care from either a hospital or hospice."

Fred said, "I wonder if Dad could stay at home on a hospice program instead of paying for the more expensive home care or nursing home beds?"

"Oh, yes," Dr. Shaw said. "I'd be happy to sign a form to get your dad on hospice right now if you wish."

"So that means you are positive he will not be alive in six months because hospice is only a six-month program?"

"Right," Dr. Shaw said. "I'm positive. I might be wrong because no one knows everything, but because there are four lesions, or a multiple tumor, and so much neurological dysfunction already and because of his age more than anything, I'm sorry to say he probably won't get the six months he wants."

(A few weeks later I called Dr. Shaw to ask more questions and thanked him for being honest with us. He said he

had decided to tell us Dad probably only had three months
to live because two of his close relatives had recently died
from cancer, and he knew how difficult it was for family
members to have no factual information on which to base
even a few plans for the future.)

I staggered out of Mayo's dark tunnels ahead of my
brother and found Tom and Dad sitting near some hedges
and flowers. I stared at Dad, who had his eyes closed and
was holding his face to the sun. Three months. I could not
believe it. I wondered if we should tell Dad what Dr. Shaw
had just said. I decided to wait till he was clearer, ready to
write, or maybe we wouldn't tell him at all. Besides, he'd
heard Dr. O'Neill say six to eleven months, and maybe he'd
make it that long. His tremendous zest for life might carry
him that far.

We drove home with Dad propped up in the middle seat
of the station wagon so that he could watch the landscape.
Fred sat in the far back talking in a low voice into his tape
recorder. We stopped to buy Dad a fish sandwich at McDonald's and a cherry pie and an apple pie. He said he'd never
been to McDonald's before. The sun was just setting and the
six-foot cornstalks threw shadows nearly thirty feet long.
Dad wasn't napping, as he had all day, but kept his eyes open,
watching the countryside, and I asked him what he was
thinking about. "It's time to get rid of the cancer and get back
to writing," he said. It was the first time he spoke of the
growth as "cancer" in my presence—and the last.

> Pa Thor rubbed his leg, and mused, "Say, I wonder, it ain't
> workin' up to a rain again, is it?"
>
> Maury smiled a little, and shook his head. "No, I don't
> think so." . . . He chuckled. "You an' your rains. You never
> forgot 'em, did y'u?"
>
> "Why!" and now the old man exploded a little and he
> came down the steps and stood beside Maury. "Why, 'course
> I ain't!"

"After all this dust, you still remember the rains?"

Pa Thor peered out toward where the horizon became vague. "Why, I kin remember the rains plain as day. Can't you?"

Maury was silent. He glanced at Kirsten, then back to Pa Thor.

Then he walked toward the barn. . . .

In the hidden country of a pilgrim's heart, rains are falling. The sun shines there, and men go into the fields and work, and believe in the work of their hands.

The Golden Bowl

Dad said he wanted to go home, but we explained that his doctors wanted him to stay in the hospital in Luverne until they could assess how the radiation treatments were going. There was a pause, and then he announced firmly, "Well, then, I want to get my wallet back."

Fred had been taking care of Dad's billfold and writing all the checks since Dad became ill, and he said, "Dad, I don't think it's a good idea. I think we should wait until you're feeling stronger."

There was another pause as I watched my father rouse himself. Surprise, then anger, sparked his blue eyes. "Now, Fred," he said, "I worked hard all my life for that billfold and for my money, and I want to have it with me!"

"But Dad, I'm worried about the hospital. It's such a public place, with people coming and going. Someone might steal the billfold or take credit cards from it while you're sleeping." Fred looked over Dad's shoulder at me, possibly for some support.

I glanced at Dad's astonished face and felt terrible so I quickly said, "All I know is when someone finds out they're very ill, it's a huge blow. Overwhelming. It's important for a person who's stuck in the hospital to keep their sense of identity, and a billfold is a big deal, a symbol of a person's identity." Dad was staring at me, and he nodded as I spoke. "Besides, I already mentioned the idea of Dad having a bill-fold to one of the nurses, and she said it was fine. She said his credit cards could be taken out and put into a safe." (Actually, it was the McKennan nurses who had said this to me at some point, but I wanted Dad to have his billfold.)

"I'd hate to have anyone get the credit cards," Fred said.

"Then keep most of the cards," Dad said, "but leave me the rest of my cards and some money and my checks."

"Dad, I don't think it's a good idea to leave blank checks around. I'm writing lots of checks for you now, and I'll never know when you've written one. The checkbook will get all mixed up again. I found a number of mistakes in that checkbook."

"The checks are mine. I've worked hard for them," Dad said.

"I think you should let Dad have some checks," I said. "It's the symbol of the billfold. It's part of . . . who a person is. It represents a person in the world."

After a pause Fred said, "Of course. I understand."

Dad gave a kingly nod. "Good," he said.

I turned around and held Dad's hand, and he held mine as if he were a little boy, trustingly, lovingly. Looking out the window at the golden fields and farmyards, he murmured every now and then, "Marvelous, marvelous," as if we were all on an exciting trip full of adventure and simple everyday hope.

As we approached Luverne, Dad said again, "I want to go home instead of back to the hospital."

And again we explained why he had to stay in the hospital for a while.

"Then I want to stop and look at my house for a minute. Is that OK, Tom?"

"Of course," Tom said, though Fred gestured at me from

behind Dad's back, indicating he didn't think this was a wise idea. We all knew how Dad liked to do what he wanted to do.

Tom drove into Dad's long driveway, and Dad stared at his house, soaking it in. " oĸ, take me inside," he said.

"We can't, Dad," I said, starting to explain again. Tom interrupted and told Dad he didn't have the strength to carry Dad inside. He said we'd come back and visit the house in a few days, with a wheelchair. Reluctantly, Dad agreed, and as we drove away he said again, "But I want my wallet back when we get to the hospital."

Fred and I made sure he had it.

Later that evening, when I was saying good-bye to Dad in the hospital, I said, "I'm glad you have your billfold and some money."

"Me, too. Check and see if it's oĸ, will you?"

I opened his bedside drawer, pulled out the wallet, and showed it to him. He held out his hand, and I gave it to him. "I'll hold it for a while," he said, enveloping it with his gigantic hands and then tucking his hands under the edge of his blankets.

"I think Fred likes to take care of money matters and does a good job of it," I said. "I'm so glad he's doing so much."

"Yes, I agree. And that's why I asked him to handle my money, but now I want to handle some of it myself. I'm a man, you know. I have some rights, even if I am in this hard place."

"I know, Dad. I'm not completely sure why Fred was resistant to the idea at first."

Dad looked at me. "Well, you know that old saying, Freya."

"What old saying?"

He smiled in the half dark. "The king is dead. The king is dead. Long live the king!"

When I told this story to Marilyn Forrest, she said, "Yes, in a way your Dad is reaping what he sowed."

"What do you mean?" I asked.

"Oh, you know his nature sometimes, so competitive, especially with other males. He wants to be number one, so at times other males will simply respond in turn. After all, he raised Fred. It wasn't the other way around."

"He's devoted to Fred," I said.

"Yes, he is," Marilyn said, "but he doesn't always show it. He was raised to treat girls differently from boys, and Fred is his only son."

> When the sun was directly overhead Flat Warclub gave the sign that they should prepare themselves for battle. Every man stripped himself down to clout and moccasins. Each man painted his face according to his battle history. Black paint and yellow paint and white paint were put on in the most fearsome manner possible. Several of the older men, Legbone and Bitten Nose and High Stomach, opened their war bundles and prayed to themselves as they removed the articles in them one by one, a bone whistle, the shell of a baby turtle, a cowrie shell, the dried feathers of what had once been a very wise crow. They told their private fetishes one by one in low singsong voices, noses quivering, eyes darting from side to side in a worshipful manner. Jaw got out his mink skin and counted over the bones of his revered uncle. He began to quiver and shake as the power of his famous warrior uncle emerged from the old yellow bones and entered his own frame.
>
> *The Manly-Hearted Woman*

Tom and I and our sons began driving back and forth to Luverne on a regular basis. We were lucky it was August. The boys were not in school, and Tom and I had no pressing writing or teaching assignments. Tom set up his computer in Dad's studio and worked on a "spec" script, and I was able to spend much of each day at the hospital. Rowan and Bly drew a huge picture of a winged green dragon with red flames coming out of its mouth to hang in Dad's hospital room. They also played basketball, watched TV, read books, and sometimes hung out with the neighbors' daughters, Susie and Katie Walgrave.

Whenever we drove back to Minneapolis, I spent half my days on the phone trying to get Dad out of the hospital and into his own house under "home care." The hospital was helping with this, but they were moving slower than I wanted. (No one could move fast enough for me.) They often did not return my calls as often or as quickly as I wished, and they sometimes forgot to follow up on my questions. Several times they told me Fred was "handling" this or that, but when I asked Fred, he said they had never mentioned it to him, and thus no progress had been made.

Then Fred and Ben Vander Kooi found an insurance policy Dad had never mentioned, which I felt would help pay for the high cost of home care. Trying to manage Dad's money carefully, Fred suggested Dad would have better care in the swing bed at the hospital, which was *free* for eighty days. I responded that Dad didn't have long to live and might soon be too ill to enjoy being home. I added that Dad should do what he wanted with his insurance money. Fred replied, sensibly enough, that Dad was so exhausted he slept most of the time anyway, so perhaps his surroundings were not that important to him. I answered that Dad had told me he wanted to go home to sleep because he could not relax as well in the hospital.

Eventually I got Dad's home care set up. I planned to spend the first two weeks looking after him myself, with moral support from Tom and the boys. After that, we'd drive down for three-day weekends and stay four days in Minneapolis to work. Fred was already doing bills, paperwork, and so many other things; I felt we should ask him to spend only one day a week at Dad's house to spell me or the rest of the helpers. I arranged for one nurse to come in from noon to eight five days a week, but I still needed to sign up several more nurses to be with Dad around the clock when Tom and I were not there.

On my next visit to Dad in the Luverne swing bed, I asked him how he was doing. "Well, honey, what with sleeping and slurping and gorging, I've dragged my butt down to the slime of the slough."

"You still want to go home?"

"You bet!"

"Well, we've arranged to get you home, and Fred has lined up people from town to drive you to radiation from there."

"Great!"

August 17 was Dad's first and last night at home. That morning Fred and I arrived at the Luverne hospital early, planning to take Dad to radiation in Sioux Falls and then home. We were excited for Dad, and he was as happy as I'd seen him for several weeks. But when we got to the hospital, we were informed that there'd been an error. Dad had been scheduled for an MRI scan the day before to see if the brain cancer was spreading to other parts of his body, but no one had taken him to the MRI truck when it arrived. Thus, we were expected to take him to the MRI lab at the Sioux Falls hospital after his radiation treatment. We knew this would be very hard on him. Radiation was already taxing the limits of his strength. Also, he detested all scans because the mild claustrophobia he'd "lived with" as a younger man had become more terrifying during his illness.

"You know, Freya, I barely got through my last scan," he said.

"What happened?"

"Oh, I had to wait for two hours to get in, and I knew ahead of time I'd feel claustrophobic once they stuck me in that tunnel, so it was sheer torture to sit in that hallway, expecting the worst. But I didn't ask for a tranquilizer because I have trouble driving home when I have those."

"How did you get through it?"

"Oh, I don't know. This young guy came in, and he took down some notes about me, and he treated me like I was some old farmer. Just because I wasn't wearing my good pants. And because I'm an older fellow, I suppose, and that's how some people treat older citizens."

"Talking down to you—"

"Exactly. So at one point I said, 'Look here, I'm Frederick Manfred, and I've written more than twenty-five novels, which is a lot more than most people have ever done, so you'd better talk kindly to me, man to man, or I'm leaving right now.'"

"What did he say to that?"

"It was hilarious, really. And sad. He went in and told the nurses I was suffering from delusions. That I mistakenly thought I was a famous author who had written all kinds of books."

"No!"

"Yes. And one of the nurses peeked out at me for a minute and started to smile to herself, and she went back in and told him I *was* a famous author."

"Then how did he behave toward you?"

"I don't know. I never saw him again. After that, the smiling nurse talked with me. She took a few more notes, and we got along just fine."

"How was the scan?"

"Every minute was sheer hell. I like big open spaces, you know. But, by God, I made it through."

> Pier turned away from the brooding hills. He himself preferred the prairie lying to the east. He looked at it. He whistled. Once again it reminded him of an ocean. It rolled away in slow gigantic waves, broadly undulating, with vast troughs running through them from north to south, as if only yesterday a storm had raged on it, and only now it was settling, calming, waves sliding into scooped-out dells, and smooth round-top hummocks replacing gray-edged slapping crests.
>
> Over all of it, riding the undulations like anchored convoys, floated separate farmyards: a red barn, a white frame house, a fading gray cattle shed, weathered outbuildings, and a budding windbreak grove of ash and maple and willow. Some farms rode the seas within call of each other; some almost out of sight.
>
> He loved the land.
>
> *This Is the Year*

We drove Dad to radiation first, and I went in with him while Fred parked the car. The radiation room was shaped like the control room of the starship *Enterprise*. Technicians stood outside glass windows pushing buttons and pulling levers while inside Dad lay on a table with a death-white mask over his head and face. The mask held him still while the radiation attacked the cancer and not the rest of his brain. He was terribly uncomfortable lying flat on his back and had trouble breathing, and three attendants could barely get him on and off the table. They said that "from now on" Dad would have to come in an ambulance on a stretcher or bring his own "lifters" to get him on and off the table. My brother and I looked at each other in dismay: it had taken some effort for Fred to find friends to drive Dad from Luverne to Sioux Falls five days a week, and now we had to find an ambulance instead, and at what cost? I felt guilty because I had lobbied for Dad to live in Luverne, which made the trip more arduous.

After radiation Dad fell asleep in his wheelchair until we wheeled him to the MRI area. There a nurse gave us a gurney so that Dad could lie down while Fred went downstairs to sign him in, and I got him some lunch. When he smelled the tuna sandwiches, Dad woke up, ate voraciously, and told me in detail how his father, Frank Feikema, had died. "I've been having long conversations with your Uncle Ed, too, since he died. And with Professor Jellema from Calvin College and others."

I looked into his eyes. "And the people you're talking with are all dead?"

"Yes. That's right. But I wish they'd all be more precise about what they are doing on the other side. Listening to them is like watching a bad TV show, badly written. I want more clarity."

"Maybe they'll get more clear with time."

"They'd better," he said, smiling, "because if they don't, pretty soon I may lose interest."

Then the nurse called us, and the MRI technicians let me stand beside Dad and pat his leg while he lay in the tunnel, using all his psychic energy to handle the waves of claustrophobia. He made it through without a tranquilizer.

As soon as we got Dad home, he crawled gratefully into his own king-size bed and fell asleep. When he woke up, he told Tom and me, matter-of-factly, how Sinclair Lewis died and how he had read the funeral oration at Lewis's funeral.

> This is the charge then: do not, while you are admiring the vapor trails fading in the firmament, while you are lamenting these his ashes still warm at our feet, do not forget that Red Lewis was human and mortal and errorful; do not forget that lights eventually burn out; do not forget that some-

one must leap forward to grab up the torch or else much that was human shall have been lost to darkness. And do not forget that any one of you, and all of you, are candidate torchbearers.

January 27, 1951. Written at Wrâlda.
"In Memoriam Address" for Sinclair Lewis
Prime Fathers

Dad also told us in great detail how Edward McDowell, his former publisher, had died, and more recently, Wallace Stegner. He spoke as if he were steadying himself and learning something by describing each man's death. "I also saw many men die in the TB sanatorium. I remember vividly when Huck Anderson died, sweet Huck Anderson. I saw this red spume erupt from his mouth, and blood was pouring down his chest. That was something for me to see from the corner of my eye."

When Tom left the room, Dad asked, "Freya, what do you suppose God will have me do when he gets me into the other place?"

"I am a little surprised to hear you ask that, Dad. I didn't know you thought there was another place."

"Well, I don't—but what will he have me do?"

"I don't know. What do you think?"

"Well, he'll need a scribe, someone to keep track of what happens there, someone who can smell and taste and feel what it's like and keep a record of it."

"Maybe that's what you'll do, Dad."

"That's right. He could have me do that job."

Later, as I was tucking him in, he said, "I don't want to float around doing nothing like some of those descriptions you hear about angels and heaven. I want an assignment."

"I can't imagine you not working, Dad."

"Me either."

He had not spoken of death before, but now, safe at

home, he could turn his considerable mental fortitude to thinking and talking about something we were all thinking about.

When he woke later in the evening, he asked me to hang Rowan and Bly's picture of the winged fire-breathing dragon on the wall of his bedroom. He spoke with great joy about how talented and handsome the boys were. "Wait till they grow up. They'll have every woman in the world chasing them. They'll be president and vice-president."

"I'm not so sure that's something to wish for, Dad."

"Oh, it will be, when they're ready. Or else, I hope at least one of them will be an artist."

He was beaming with pleasure, delighted to play host in his own comfortable home. He asked Tom and me to draw chairs up to the bed and eat dinner with him, which we did. The boys came in to say hi, and Dad told them he was going to start working upstairs in his studio "by next week." He fell asleep and woke again at eleven after "an incredible sleep" and had ice cream and cookies and went back to sleep, saying, "If any pretty girls come by and want to see me, scoot them in here, will you?" When I temporarily couldn't find his favorite little down pillow and told him I couldn't recall where I had last seen it, he joked, "Well, this thing I've got wrong with me must be catching."

> He found it hard to die.
>
> He threshed out blindly. He fought. He wriggled against the dark, deadly undertow. His mind became a kettle simmering with escaping fear. Huge yellow-red fires burst open in his eyes. He cried. He choked. All the frozen-flesh rocks of the world seemed to be holding him down. The stiff water bound his hands.
>
> Then his head shot clear of the water. He threshed the air, threw up a high arm, gulped gallons of fresh air. The hot summery air of July was as sweet as rain water.

The rocks towered above him, steep.

He flailed his long arms, churning the water. He cursed himself for not having learned to swim well in his youth. He splashed. He was a spastic crab throwing out wild limbs. He hurried to get to the side before the gigantic red-rock mouth closed over him again.

Before him rose the Devil's Stairway, its irregular cracks and flat platform slabs of rock leading to the prairie above. With fright-powered effort Pier heaved himself out of the water, gained the first ledge. He scrambled upward. His heart thumped. He climbed up the stairway, grabbing onto cedar roots, fern stems, flat rocks. He rushed out of the abyss, out of the maw of eternity.

This Is the Year

The next morning Becky Bunkers, the home-care administrative nurse, came by to go over the details of Dad's schedule. We charted who would be with him every hour of every day. She said that if things went well, Dad would be stronger after radiation, and we would be able to cut down on his care. She gave me a list of his medications and when he had to take them. It was more than a page long, and there were more than twenty different pills to be taken at different times. Then she gave Dad a physical exam, showing me how to check his blood sugar (he had become diabetic) and his pulse. She said he seemed to be doing pretty well, but she noticed "some congestion" in his lungs and said she'd speak to the doctors about it. When she heard how much trouble Tom was having getting Dad to the toilet on the walker, she promised to have a wheelchair sent out to us "within a week."

"Try to make that sooner," Tom said.

"I'll try," she said, "but it may take a week."

A few hours after she left, Fred arrived. It was time to

drive Dad to radiation again. Just as we were leaving the phone rang, and we were informed that Dad had to go back to the Sioux Falls MRI facility after his radiation treatment because the technicians had made some kind of error the day before. It was so hard to break that news to Dad; he was tired, and he'd thought the MRIs were over forever.

This time Fred stood next to Dad during the scan, patting his leg and talking to help him get through the experience without tranquilizers. Although the technicians told us it would take "twenty minutes at the very most" to make up for their mistake the day before, Dad lay in the dark tunnel with Fred standing beside him for more than an hour. After each scan Dad said, "That's enough now. I need to get back home." Once he said, "I can't stay in this place anymore. I have to get out." Each time the technicians told Dad he had only "ten minutes more," or "seven minutes more," but each time he came out, more minutes were added. Dad was exhausted, and his face had turned white. Fred and I were furious, and at one point, after Dad had been inside the steel tunnel for an hour and fifteen minutes, Fred waited until the clicking and knocking from the scan had stopped, and then shouted, "That's it now! No more! We're leaving!"

"One more and we're done," a technician said.

"No more!" Fred shouted.

But we stayed for one more. Dad looked as if he were dying. The whole situation felt like an exercise in futility. We couldn't imagine what difference it made at this point whether Dad had cancer elsewhere in his body or not. If the cancer had spread, he would have been too weak to survive further treatment for it. (Within a few days we were told the MRI showed no cancer anywhere else in his body.)

After the MRI, still angry, Fred stayed behind to see if the technicians would tell him who had made the mistake that cost Dad so much time and energy. Desperate to make Dad's life happier, I rolled him to the cafeteria and bought him two chocolate yogurt cones, even though he wasn't supposed to have sugar. Then I rolled him outside into the August sunshine.

"This is better, right, Dad?"

"Yes. I love being outside."

"When we get home we can open the sliding door to your bedroom, and the sun will shine on your bed."

"I know. I look forward to that. But right now I'm so tired I could sleep for a week."

"I'm so angry you had to go through this again."

"Me, too," Dad said. "Except I'm too tired to feel angry."

Luckily Fred arrived within moments, and, as we were rolling Dad to his car, I suggested to Fred that we steal a wheelchair. Since the last thing I stole in my life was in graduate school, when I took a can of corn from a Palo Alto Safeway (and left the money for it a week later when I got paid), I was quite surprised at how I'd suddenly turned into a thief. I was so angry about the MRI mix-up and my feelings of helplessness so overwhelmed me that I wanted some power. I also felt a sense that the world owed something to my father—now!

As soon as the words were out of my mouth, Fred was in on the scheme. After helping Dad into the car, Fred simply walked back to the front of the hospital, grabbed one of the wheelchairs, and wheeled it into the parking lot, where I met him with the car. Fred opened the trunk, folded the chair into it, and hopped into the backseat.

"Got it," he said.

"Good," I said and took off. All the way home I imagined that the police were after us and practiced explaining why in the world we'd been stupid enough to steal a wheelchair. All of my excuses sounded lame, and I knew Dad would never approve as he was always meticulously honest. But he was staring off over the cornfields, half dozing, and he didn't seem to realize what we'd done.

We let Fred off in Luverne and drove on toward Roundwind. Dad began talking again about death: "Cousin Alice [Feikema] told me I was lucky that Uncle Ed went when he did. Because you don't want someone hanging on like that, an endless weight and a burden to others. At first I wasn't sure she was right, because I missed Ed, but Alice was right."

When we got back to Roundwind, Dad was so depleted we could not get him out of the car, which we drove down the precarious slope in front of the house and parked by his bedroom. Tom used the walker to drag Dad part of the short ten feet to the house, but he finally sagged to the ground outside the sliding glass door, unable to help move himself. He lay on his back, blinking up at the sun. "Don't worry, this is fine," he said, panting a little. "The fresh air feels nice on my face."

"Well, you can't stay here all night, Dad."

"Maybe I can," he said, craning his neck to gaze around at the tall prairie grass. "Get me a blanket, and I can rest awhile."

I deeply wanted to do just that. I could lie beside him, and we'd eat now and then and chat and maybe have a bonfire, and eventually he'd die out under the stars.

Tom and I called Rowan and Bly to help us. Again and again, Tom and the boys tried to lift Dad but sank under his weight. Rowan was near tears, and Bly looked both angry and terrified. Tom looked at me in dismay.

"Hey!" I said. "I know what! I just stole a wheelchair from McKennan Hospital!"

"You're kidding," Tom said. "Where is it?"

I pointed triumphantly. "In the trunk of the car."

"Thank God," Tom said as he and the boys unfolded the chair, dragged Dad into it, and, using all their strength, got him across five more feet of grass and five feet of carpeting and into his bed. If we'd had no wheelchair, I suppose he would have lain on the ground until we called an ambulance. (Feeling guilty about our heist, we returned the wheelchair a few days later.)

Dad had a sandwich, but he could not sleep. He stopped talking in a clear and candid way about death and began to babble in a more confused fashion about his brother John's death and Ed's death and his mother's death. He was having difficulty breathing again. I tried to calm him by stroking his face and hands, but he began to look around the room, seeing things that were not there. He plucked at imaginary things in the air and "ate" them, telling us he was enjoying "some bread and cream." Then he began eating his blue blanket. "You ought to try it, Freya, it's half animal and half vegetable but better tasting than either. It's even better than ice cream or johnnycake."

After a moment I decided to be frank. "Dad, that's your blue blanket you're trying to eat."

He smiled. "I'm aware that you know it's my blanket. But right now, Freya, it's more than a blanket to me."

I called the hospital, and they said, "Bring him in."

"He can't walk," I said.

So they sent the ambulance, and thus ended Dad's last day at home. It was also the last time he saw his home. And the last time he spoke about death (with me at least) until two days before he died.

> Pier tore into two clumps of wood that he had tried to split all last winter. His ax swung, rang, exploded splinters.
>
> He paused, breathing hoarsely. His eyes fastened on the flashing blade. He lifted the ax, felt of its heft. How easily it could pop open a skull.
>
> Nertha seemed to think it was hard dying. She was wrong. Death was easy, had always been easy, had always been breathing on his neck.
>
> He dropped the ax into the wood. Could death come

now, now, at this minute, it would end all sorrows, erase all
hurt, cut guilt from the heart, blast the heart to hell.
This Is the Year

Back at the hospital they put Dad on oxygen, and he
breathed better. After running a series of tests, they began
to treat him for sepsis and what they called "infiltration of
the lung." Sepsis kills fifty percent of those who get it, which
we were not told at the time. But I did know about pneumonia and about Dad's weak lungs because of his history of
tuberculosis.

The next morning I spoke with the doctor who had taken
over for Dr. Kuiper for two weeks. "Does 'infiltration of the
lung' mean pneumonia?"

"Not quite," he said. "We don't want to call it that yet."

I felt bad seeing Dad back in the hospital. "Sorry, Dad.
I wish you could have stayed home longer."

"Don't worry," he said. "The radiance [he always called
the radiation therapy 'the radiance'] is clearing off my lymphoma, though it's making me sluggish. But I walked down
the hall with my walker today, and I stood up straight. So I'll
get back home in a week or so to finish my book."

I checked with the nurses to be absolutely sure, and they
said no, Dad had not walked, could not walk, could not even
go to the bathroom by himself. He was "fairly oriented" but
now and then "delusional." He was not good at controlling
his hands and arms, and Fred had to rotate his watch and
turn on the TV for him. That night Dad said, "You know,
Freya, I have no regrets." Then a smile, "Of course sometimes I can't think well enough to know if I have regrets."

I said, "You did the best you could, that's why."

"Yes," he said.

Over the next two and a half weeks Dad went steadily downward, with intermissions, as a great tree falls in the forest,
arrested and supported briefly by smaller trees, but finally

continuing the inevitable, gravity-bound journey toward earth. He continued going to Sioux Falls for radiation, now in a stretcher in an ambulance so he slept most of the way. Once the technicians were late for the appointment, so they drove eighty-five miles an hour to Sioux Falls. "Absolutely irresponsible," my brother fumed.

For the first time Dad began to speak negatively every day about being in the hospital. "Freya, I don't care for this place. It's hard. The furniture is hard, the bed is hard, the food is hard. The people are hard, too, though they try their best."

"I know, Dad. I'm still doing everything I can to get you home. But the doctor says we have to wait until the antibiotic clears out the sepsis."

"But I can't eat what I want and sleep when I need to. I want to go home. Why do you think the doctor is holding me down?"

"I think, from a medical point of view, the doctor is honestly trying to help you," I answered.

"But he's not allowing for more expression of who I am," Dad said. "I'm not used to him." The doctor substituting for Dr. Kuiper was thoroughly professional: hardworking, conscientious, concerned, careful, and always trying to stay clearheaded about the complex list of things going wrong with Dad. But I wasn't used to him either, and I had trouble feeling allied with him. He entered the room, asked a few questions of the nurses, and, if pressed, gave a few opinions to Dad or me. He left without conveying any sense that we were all in this together and without asking whether Dad or I might have any comments. He put Dad on the most narrowly appropriate antibiotic for the sepsis and kept taking X-rays to see how Dad's lungs were. Dad had to skip radiation for several days because he was too exhausted from fighting the sepsis, a bladder infection, and the "infiltration." Then he went back to radiation, got tired out again, and rallied once more. I felt he would be dead within a month, although the doctor carefully avoided either agreeing or disagreeing with my feelings.

> The terrible feeling that life was slowly unraveling out from under him, that, worse yet, he could do nothing about it, moved over him like a great storm cloud. Life was falling apart, it was all slipping away from him, and he could do nothing to stop it. Calamity was coming down on him like a sliding rockfall falling down on a man already pinned to earth. No matter what desperate measures he might take, no matter how he might jack first one way and then the other, in the end, finally, he was doomed, and no longer would he be around to enjoy his green meadow and life beside the Shaken Grass.
>
> Then he rallied. Like a grizzly tormented into one last desperate lunge and bite, his animal came up and rose terrible in the back of his head, rampant. His eyes opened terrible under his dark brows, glowed like balls of silverish fire. His carven walnut face set rock hard. Who was Hunt or Mitch or Jesse or any of the hired killers to cow, even kill, a Hammett? He was a grandson of the great Gramp Hammett. All his life he'd had to hold his wild one in check for fear of going too far, of hurting someone, of overstroking when a light stroke would serve. Here now was a chance to let it out full force without having to worry about hurting the good. The odds were more than equal at last. A young army was out there to get him and he now had the right to fight with all he had. And he would. They might get him, but he would get some of them too, a lot of them.
>
> He made another round of the windows, placing shots where he thought the killers might be hiding.
>
> *Riders of Judgment*

My father never felt like a burden, although I sometimes allowed other relatives to burden me, and sometimes I was a burden to myself. Mostly, I deeply appreciated being with him in the hospital. His speech was garbled at times, but usually he said wonderful things. He was curious to the end, with a sweet disposition, unblaming and uncomplaining and even reassuring. Whenever he had a setback, he'd look at my face and say, "It will be all right, Dolly. Don't worry, it will be all right."

And to Rowan and Bly he said, "It will be all right, Dollies, don't worry. I don't like you to see your grandpa like this because I want you to remember me as strong and writing. And I'll be back writing, too, in just a few days."

> Suddenly he saw a white mare coming toward him, trotting lightly, shaking her curly mane, whisking her long tail. She was so glistening white he could not look directly at her. She was whiter than sun on snow on a bright winter morning. Also a halo of whiteness hovered about her. The whiteness cast a dazzling sheen on all things near her, the rocks, the rosebushes, the silver sage. She was a holy being, a great and mysterious one, incomprehensible, wakan. She neighed lightly. Gaily she lifted her tail. Watching her closely he saw she had reddish lips and blue eyes. She smiled at him in a secret way.
>
> The hair on his head stiffened. His heart jumped wildly.
>
> The white mare stood over him. Holding her head to one side, she looked down at him. "Are you afraid, my son?"
>
> The moment he heard her voice he felt calm. "I no longer fear."
>
> *Conquering Horse*

I called Carol Bly, an old friend of Dad's, and asked her if she knew of anyone with a literary background who might want a job as a full-time nurse. (I figured that a nurse who loved books would be more fun for Dad, who still enjoyed discussing books and writing.) Carol suggested that I ask the fledgling Luverne hospice program if they would have adequate morphine or other drugs to stop Dad's pain at the end, if needed. She said to make sure that the hospice workers who attended Dad had "the guts" to handle another person's dying and pain. Then she commented on Dad's "springy attitude" toward life. "If I were God," she said, "I'd send Fred Manfred back to earth to show everyone that cheer and curiosity are an act of will. Rather than moaning and groaning over things, he set his mind, his will, to staying cheerful and curious about life."

And Margaret Sonja Luitjens, wife of LeRoy Luitjens, the Luverne contractor who helped Dad build Roundwind, said, in her German English, "Your Dad is the simplest guy I have ever known. My daughter-in-law bought one of his books. I don't know how many of his books she's read, but do you know they even got that baseball book—what's the name of it, *Baseball*, or something [*No Fun on Sunday*]. They got that down there as far as Oklahoma where she lives, and she never had one signed, and she went to the hospital, and your dad ... my gosh ... he couldn't talk but he still could sign it there in the hospital. Yes, your dad is the most simplest guy I have ever known." Of course she meant "simplest" in the sense of the Shaker hymn, " 'Tis a gift to be simple, 'tis a gift to be free."

Tom and I and the boys drove home for a few days. Less than a day after we got home, Dad's right lung collapsed in a spontaneous pneumothorax and had to be inflated again by Dr. Gutnik, a thoracic surgeon called in from Rock Rapids, Iowa. The procedure was done without anesthesia, which they didn't think Dad could survive. I spoke to Dr. Gutnik by phone a few hours after he inflated the lung, and his first words to me were, "Your poor dad. What a great guy." He indicated, somehow without saying it, that Dad had only a few weeks to live. "Your dad's natural enthusiasm and energy for life make him seem more well to everyone than he actually is." Dr. Gutnik was a perceptive man.

We raced back to Luverne and found Dad lying in bed with a tube draining large amounts of blood and pus from his right lung into a container on the floor. Every time he moved his right arm or tried to shift to a slightly different position, the drainage tube "stuck" him, and he sucked in a sudden breath of pain. The room smelled terrible, and I kept opening a window to ease the odor as well as to please Dad, who said he liked to "hear the birds and eavesdrop on the kids who bicycle by."

Dr. Kuiper—oh, that welcome face—was back from vacation, and he called a family conference with Tom, Fred, and me. His face was grave. He said that he had expected to find Dad at home, going to radiation five times a week with friends or family, sleeping a lot, and slowly recovering. Instead, he found Dad "really sunk down low," and he added that he, too, felt Dad had "a few weeks at most to live." Fred and Tom and I asked if there was much point to dragging our exhausted father to radiation anymore since he couldn't even sit up straight in bed and had to be propped with pillows. Dr. Kuiper said that the tumor had probably shrunk a great deal, and he would talk to the Mayo Clinic about continuing radiation. In the meantime, radiation was canceled.

I begged to take Dad home. "If Dad's not going to be on radiation, he can go home under hospice care."

"When Dr. Gutnik takes out the tube draining the pus from his right lung, he can probably do that," Dr. Kuiper said.

"Why can't we take the tube and the whole works home?" I asked.

"Because the tube has to be X-rayed every day to see if it's in place and working to drain the lung. The X-ray machines weigh thousands of pounds, and we can't bring them up to your dad's house. Nor can your dad be driven in each day, as no one can get him into a wheelchair or out of bed anymore."

"What are the chances the tube may never come out?" I asked.

"Fifty-fifty," Dr. Kuiper said.

"I want to take Dad home even with the tube, if that becomes necessary. He asks me every day to get him home. Dad is an amazing person. He's very sensitive, and I believe he, of all people, needs to die in his own home."

"I don't usually allow a patient to go home in his condition," Dr. Kuiper said, "but I see your point. Your father is strong minded and sensitive at the same time. That's a hard combination when you're in a hospital. There is no question he'd be better at home, despite my bending the rules to get him there."

Dr. Kuiper added that if he'd not been on vacation when Dad developed sepsis, he might have considered the possibility of letting Dad "go," letting him die, by withholding the rare and expensive antibiotic for the sepsis.

"Why would you have considered that route?" Tom wondered.

"Because this type of antibiotic is so hard on the body it can likely kill him by itself; it's so difficult to get and so expensive and so unusual that it is in some ways equivalent to using a breathing machine as a last-ditch effort to keep someone alive. And your dad has been very clear that he never wanted to be on a breathing machine."

I was so eager to get Dad home to die in peace that I called Dr. O'Neill at the Mayo Clinic and asked if he had any ideas of how to get Dad home. Dr. O'Neill said he was "sorry to hear such a neat guy was having such a bad time." He added that "sepsis plus a bladder infection plus possible pneumonia are all life-threatening and life-ending in themselves for an eighty-two-year-old man, and the real danger now is not the tumor, which has probably been considerably reduced, but the infectious diseases: sepsis and pneumonia."

> He tried to imagine what it would be like to have the sun come up on the eastern horizon, fresh and beaming and ennobling, coming upon the world, and he not there to welcome it with his flame. It could not be! Were he to go tonight, there would be clouds in the morning. There would be clouds. The universe would sorrow for him. The spheres of heaven would wail. The moon would weep inconsolably for him. The sun would warm the world in vain.
>
> He stared at the west wing's roof. A day had gone.
>
> With a cry he burst upward in bed, sitting erect; and by his action raised the level of his vision to a point where he could once more catch a glimpse of his golden friend. He could see only a sliver of it, but it was good, and golden.
>
> Again, slowly, inexorably, it sank out of sight.
>
> With the desperate anxiety of an animal trapped in closing jaws, he pushed his body upward from his white bed, and again, miraculously, saw his sun!
>
> But, still it fell.
>
> He stood up, tottering, gripping the window frame, gripping it with a mighty effort, gripping it to keep from falling. He coughed. He gasped for breath. Once more he caught a flame.
>
> *Boy Almighty*

A few days later Dad rallied, and Dr. Kuiper took him off acute care and put him back into a swing bed. The difference was that Medicare paid for every day he spent hospitalized in acute care but only eighty days of hospitalization in a swing bed. In the swing bed the nurses didn't check on Dad's vital signs as frequently or help him with his food and general care as much. Dad said, "I prefer swing bed because I hate to bother the nurses." Also, once a patient was in a swing bed, the hospital expected him or her to move to a nursing home as soon as possible. In fact, twenty minutes after Dr. Kuiper's substitute had moved Dad from acute care to a swing bed some weeks earlier, a member of the hospital staff began pressuring us to get Dad out of the hospital because we had only "a few days left on Medicare with the swing bed." When Fred explained to her that Dad still had eighty days left, she checked some files and stopped talking about it. But now Dr. Kuiper felt Dad had "come back for good," since "almost all" the sepsis was gone. We just had to wait for the tube to stop draining blood and pus from his lung, and we could either take him home or find him a nursing home.

Uncle Henry and Uncle Floyd and their families came to visit, as did Dad's friends Waring Jones, John Rezmerski, Bill Holm, Art Huseboe, and Wayne Knutson. Aunt Ellen, Henry's wife, later told me that during their visit with him Dad suddenly said, "You know, Henry, I've got to get this right."

Unsure what Dad was referring to, Henry asked, "Get it right? Get *what* right?"

"Dying," Dad answered. "You get one chance to do it right. This is my only chance."

Waring Jones wanted to read to Dad from *Lord Grizzly* but reported that Dad didn't seem interested in listening. Waring told me that years before when his father was dying in a hospital in Minneapolis, Waring had read *Lord Grizzly* to him, and they'd enjoyed it together during some of the last meaningful hours they shared. Waring was right; Dad didn't care to be read to, unless it was a short card or a letter from a friend. Nor did he care to listen to the music tapes Marya left for him because the earplugs "bothered" his ears. "It's too much," he said. But he still watched the TV news and struggled to stay awake until 8:00 one evening to watch Barbra Streisand's concert for President Clinton's mother. When it turned out Barbra didn't appear on the Luverne

Hospital channels, Dad watched the three tenors instead, Luciano Pavarotti, Plácido Domingo, and José Carreras. He lay smiling, drifting in and out of sleep, murmuring, "Marvelous, marvelous."

Dad had been back in a swing bed for one day when he was joined by his first and only roommate, an elderly farmer from Hills, who hated the TV shows Dad enjoyed, didn't like the window open, and had chatting relatives constantly visiting him. My conversations with Dad could now be overheard, so I enjoyed my visits with him less. I asked Dad if he felt equally disgruntled by the presence of his new roommate. "Should I see if the nurses can move him to another room?"

"Oh, no," Dad said. "Let him be. I like having company at night, if not in the day. Besides, I enjoy eavesdropping on his conversations with his relatives. It's good material for my novels."

The next day, one of the new roomie's visitors shuffled over to Dad's bed and stood with his face one foot above my father's sleeping face. Before I realized what he was doing or could stop him, he rasped, "Fred Manfred? Are you Mr. Manfred?"

"Uh . . . yes, that's me," Dad said, blinking his eyes open.

"Well, Mr. Manfred, I have something very important to tell you."

"What's that?" Dad said.

"Because of what you write in your books, Mr. Manfred, and because you decided to leave God's church, you're going straight to hell when you die!"

"To hell?!" Dad said, opening his eyes farther.

I stood up then and waved the man away, but he ignored me. "Yes, Mr. Manfred! I know the Bible and I live by the Bible, but you do not, and now you are going straight to hell to pay for your sins!"

"My sins?" Dad said.

"Yes! Writing all those books with so much evil in them!"

"That's enough!" I said. "Please leave."

"Straight to hell!" the old man said, his mouth even closer to Dad's face.

"Well, now," Dad said, trying to pull himself together. "I don't know about that . . . You see—"

The man interrupted. "Yes! Straight to hell! I know it!"

"I want you to leave now," I said to the man.

"Pardon me?" he said, looking up.

"You have to leave. You're bothering my father. If you don't leave right now, I will make you leave." I stepped toward the man until I touched his arm and gave it a small push. "I want you to get out, now!"

A nurse bobbed in. "Is this man bothering Mr. Manfred?"

"Yes, he is," I said.

"Oh, dear, we cannot allow that," she said. She took the man's arm. "Sir, you have to leave. Come on."

The man followed the nurse out of the room, and my father said to me, "Well, Freya, you didn't have to do that."

"Yes, I did," I said. "I hate him. Who does he think he is?"

"He's a lost soul," my father said, "and I hate to bother the nurses about him. Besides, he wasn't that bad."

"He woke you up!"

"I know, I know, but he's an ignorant person, Freya. There are a lot of them around here. I don't like to say so, but there are a lot of them."

"That doesn't make me feel any better!"

"Well, you're like a grizzly bear with cubs," my father said.

"You bet! He has no right to disturb you!"

My father smiled. "Well, at least I know I'm safe now."

During the first four weeks of Dad's illness, I rarely got depressed because I was busy doing all I could for him and also because I hoped he could buy two or three months of good writing time with radiation. But in the last weeks I began to feel that there was a fate worse than death and Dad was living it. He was not in great pain, but the drainage tube hurt him with each movement—"A nagging, stabbing feeling," he said. He could only take Tylenol for relief because he was taking so many other drugs.

I wanted to give him one last gift. He asked me to take him home almost every day, and I wanted to. Even his doctor said he'd be better off. But the logistic difficulties seemed insurmountable. Luverne was just starting a hospice program, and the guidelines for assistance offered at that time were still being determined, still at a fledgling status. When Tom and I first spoke with several hospice personnel, they gave us guidelines that they said were "only temporary" but the best they could do. (Luverne has since established an extensive, full-scale hospice system.) They told us that Dad was in the "category" of being "cured by radiation," and therefore he was not dying. Thus, "technically" hospice could not assist him. They explained that for the same reason Medicare would not support home care: radiation is considered a "cure," and a person "can't be dying and getting Medicare to pay for radiation at the same time." When I mentioned to them that Dr. Shaw at Mayo had told Fred and me that he would sign a form for hospice care even while Dad was getting radiation, they said that was "good news" and that perhaps he could go home on hospice. But there were a few more catches, which I jotted down while Tom asked further questions:

1. Hospice could provide four hours of free care per day as well as help us find twenty more hours of care elsewhere, paid for by the family. The beginning hospice program could only manage this for a month, "at the most." Kindly,

they asked, "What if your father lives longer than a month? What sort of care will you turn to then?"

2. Because Dr. Kuiper had taken Dad off acute care and placed him in a swing bed, he now had only thirty days to stay home on hospice before he had to return to swing bed status, or else he'd lose eighty free days of swing bed paid for by his extra insurance. Thus, when or if he returned to the hospital, he'd pay nearly two hundred dollars a day for hospital care.

3. There was one scenario that would work perfectly: if Dad happened to go from hospice care at home into acute care at the hospital, he could keep his eighty free days at the hospital, and there would be no problem. But could we convince Dr. Kuiper to redesignate Dad's position as acute rather than swing, if it should happen that Dad moved from hospice back to the Luverne hospital?

4. Caring for Dad at home involved other pros and cons, which the hospice personnel covered with us in detail: *(a)* Could we get a stretcher to move him to our car so that we could drive him home? The hospital could not afford the ambulance. *(b)* It would take two people to bathe him at home. *(c)* He'd have to use diapers and bedpans. *(d)* A hospice nurse would have to stay with him all night when I was not with him, but I still hadn't found one who could do this. *(e)* Food would "probably taste better" at home, but who would purchase it on a regular basis and get it to his caretakers when I was not able to do it? Fred said he was worried it might be him. *(f)* Pain control would be better at home, with "more moment-to-moment care," and "patches" that released pain medication into the bloodstream, if need be. Plus, if problems arose, there was free backup from a registered nurse even

on weekends. *(g)* Dad had to sit up every day, and it already took four nurses to get him in an upright position. How would we manage this at home? *(h)* He'd need an oxygen tank in his bedroom because he used it full time in the hospital. Oxygen would be paid for by hospice. *(i)* Fred was worried the nurses would call him all the time about how to run Dad's house when I wasn't there: electricity, water, lights, heat, whatever.

Every morning when I visited him, Dad told me his dreams. "Last night I had so many dreams. I was battling all kinds of people. A bunch of ghosts came and told me I had to save the arts for America. But all kinds of people were trying to stop me from doing this, pontificating and reading their endless papers: congressmen, some businessmen, and some other loud people from every state of the Union. So, to get even, I pooped on their stupid papers. For three whole weeks I felt so satisfied because I pooped on their stupid papers."

Another morning he said, "I was going to parties all night long, some up on Blue Mound. Allen Tate was there and all kinds of other literary types, people I love: good food, good talk, discussing politics, and dancing, too. The worst was when thousands of Swedes in their big Cadillacs filled with jewels and food came from across the sea. They weren't invited, but there they came. No one knew what to do. There were no instructions what to do with all these fat cats. You had to hang around by yourself and do the best you could. But after a while it got better. The fat cats couldn't ruin our party, no matter how they tried."

> The drums gathered them all together, Chippewa and Sioux. . . .
>
> Swirling, bounding, they danced with passionate abandon. Some darted like streaking wolves. Some hopped like robins and pulled up imaginary worms. Some came swoop-

ing like eagles and caught up soft rabbits. Some rushed and gored like buffalo bulls. Some charged like elk bulls. Some stalked like foxes. Around and through and around they whirled. Hoops twirled, war shields revolved, lances rode high. And at last, slowly out of the melee rose an added frenzy, a transforming ecstacy. They became their own incarnations. A green prairie had suddenly brought forth new creatures. They sang. They cried. They leaped.

Arrow of Love

Dad was very upset because he imagined an old woman schoolteacher was asking him to wrap tiny gift packages for some schoolchildren. "Are the packages all ready?" he'd ask. "Are they all lined up? If I don't have packages for all of the children, the schoolteacher will be very angry!"

"What schoolteacher, Dad?"

"Can you imagine," he said to me, with his teeth bared in disgust. "I've written more than thirty books, and I'm eighty-two years old, and she expects me to find and wrap presents for everyone! Can you believe the gall of this woman?"

Then he'd anxiously start wrapping packages in midair with his fingers trembling, his eyes fearful.

After two or three similar discussions, I finally told him the packages were all wrapped—that I'd seen to it myself, and the schoolteacher had gone away totally satisfied. He said, "Oh that's good news. That's really good news." And he never mentioned her again.

Another time, after Mom had visited him, he asked me, "What did you think about Maryanna when you saw her last night?"

"She seemed OK. What did *you* think?"

"I thought she was switching from one topic to the next pretty fast. I couldn't follow her. It seemed like her brain was tracking too fast."

A few hours later Clarence Feikema, a relative, strode into the room to shake hands with Dad. Dad became instantly alert and happy. "Clarence!"

"I came to see how you were doing, Fred!"

"Oh, well, I ran out of brains," Dad said.

"You had more than most to start with," Clarence said, smiling.

"I ran out of them, too," Dad said.

One morning he concentrated on his five brothers. "I have real loyal brothers, but I really miss Ed."

"I know, Dad. Abben called last night from California."

"I know," he said, smiling at the thought of his brother. "That Abben. What a guy. He was always singing and whistling on the yard. You should have seen him. Mainly he was an honest guy, kind and cheerful and a good worker."

"What about Floyd?"

"Oh, we had a couple of tussles, and Pa sometimes favored him. Pa told him to tear the Ford apart that was on our yard, and I didn't care for that. Floyd always had such a good manner about him, his behavior at table and such. He never complained. And you should have seen him play baseball. What a talent he had. He was and is a very strong man."

"And what about Henry?"

"Oh, I like Henry a great deal because I always had a good time with him. I never once had a bad time or wished I wasn't around him. We could talk until after midnight. He has a cheerful smile. He's a very strong man, physically and emotionally. When he tries to do something he does it thoroughly. He's honest. He never burned me once. He's a first-rate brother."

The weekend before Labor Day I felt strongly that Dad was too sick for a swing bed. He needed acute care. He couldn't sit up without asking to lie down a moment later. Once when the nurses helped him to an armchair and left him for a while, Tom and Fred and I found him folded forward with his chin flat against his knees, eyes staring down at the floor, unable to straighten himself. When I told the nurses, they said they'd have to find some other way to "get him sitting up a little bit each day."

He told me, "You wouldn't believe what goes on here at the hospital all night. Now there are only a few patients left here, and lots of doctors and nurses with less to do. So they play around and fool around here all night long, laughing and partying and talking. And they flirt with each other. I've no proof, but I can hear them. At the same time they are very helpful. They say prayers for you."

"Prayers?"

"One of their prayers goes like this, 'No, no, no, no, no, no, no, no, no,' and each 'no' is said with a different inflection. That's a very beautiful one, that No Prayer, and one of their favorites. I have to admit the rhythm is pretty good."

He asked me several times if I could see the woman in bed beside him. I didn't know what to say. "Do you see someone in bed with you, Dad?"

"Yes, she's right here next to me."

"Is she nice or not nice?" I asked, fearful that the demanding schoolteacher had returned.

"Oh, nice and very lovely," he said.

"Good," I said. "Then I'm glad she's there."

"You bet," he said, and smiled happily.

I had not watched a loved one die before. Because of Dad's occasional hallucinations and exhaustion, it seemed to me he had days, maybe only hours, left. But some of my friends and some of the nurses said, "Your dad could go on for months this way." I began to feel glad there *was* a tumor that would kill him eventually because he was too miserable and ill to walk, sit, or write. He could barely talk and only roused himself when he wanted to with all his heart or when he felt duty-bound and obliged. It reassured me to know that even if he went into a nursing home, it would not be for two years, but for a much shorter time.

> To see life slowly vanish from the nomad bones of his father was to see that there was no such thing as death per se. Death, Thurs decided, was only the absence of life. Death was only a vague term people used to describe an unknown on either side of what little life men got. When men thought they were witnessing the approach of what they called death, they were merely seeing the fleeing of life. And once life vanished there was nothing left except a few bewildered cancer cells and other parasitic organisms. After that came clusters of marvelously multiplying bacteria, then some molecular activity, then loose atoms. To see the life of his father slowly vanish was to see the gates of earth set ajar, was to see ties and connections never seen before.
>
> *Wanderlust*

One sunny day outside the hospital, Fred and I disagreed even more openly about what to do next. We were both tired. I was feeling low, and I imagine Fred might have been low as well, but I didn't ask him. Fred said he didn't want Dad to go home on hospice for the following reasons:

1. Dad would want his billfold back and might want to make out checks himself. He had made a number of mistakes on his checkbook before he got sick and might do so again. (Fred says in retrospect his state of mind may have been based on the knowledge that Dad had very little money.)

2. It would cost around two hundred dollars a day to have Dad at home, whereas the hospital was still free for a month or more.
3. Dad would have better care in the hospital and less pain at the end of his life. Though Fred was and is a veteran hospice volunteer with a firm belief in the hospice system, especially for the emotional aspect of the care they give, he was thinking of the benefits of the many actual physical services in the hospital versus what hospice volunteers could bring to the home.
4. Dad would get less intensive physical therapy at home, compared to the hospital.

I argued that mistakes in a checkbook were not important at this point, that the two hundred dollars a day was Dad's money, not ours. Besides, the hospice people Tom and I had spoken with assured me Dad's care would be better at home because there would be one person with him every minute of the day, and he would not lie or sit alone for hours as he sometimes did with the hospital swing bed care. They also said he would not have to beg for pain relief from the caretakers and then wait for them to consult the doctors before they gave him Tylenol. (Thankfully, the only pain relief Dad asked for was something to ease the stabbing of the tube sticking into his back. His cancer caused him no pain.) Finally, I wondered how much physical therapy a dying man could benefit from. I added that three friendly nurses from the hospital had told me, one by one, that Dad should "go home to die" and not stay in the hospital.

I didn't mention how many times Dad asked me to take him home and how earlier that day he'd said, "Whether you get someone to help or not, Freya, I want to go home. You can take care of me." When I answered that Tom and I could handle it for a longer time if we had some backup ready, he said, "You can do it. That's what daughters do." As he said these words, I knew that he meant that he was dying and that he wanted me to get him home so I could help him die in the right place.

My father seemed to see Fred and me quite differently, and his varying expectations sometimes placed my brother and me at odds. When Fred entered the room, Dad's face brightened, and he chatted about the Vikings or about whether Fred was playing catch with Rowan and Bly, or he turned serious to ask about the mail or money matters. Their relationship reflected the fun they'd had together as "guys" and also Fred's "brotherly" or almost "fatherly" chores and responsibilities on Dad's behalf. When I entered the room, Dad's face warmed, and he became more emotional, discussing his feelings about doctors, nurses, the hospital, and all sorts of other people living and dead. Our relationship reflected his need for "mothering" or "sistering," which was more closely aligned with caretaking. It seemed to be my job to get him home (with Tom's "bull-like" assistance all the way) and stay with him.

Then Fred said he "hadn't wanted to tell" me, but the stress of Dad's dying had placed him in a position where he truly couldn't take it any more—and that he had developed an ulcer. He felt his ulcer would get worse if Dad went home, partly, he said, because he'd have to drive out every day to see Dad and to provide physical and emotional care. He feared his responsibilities would increase if Dad left the hospital, especially as he was the only relative living in the area. Since I'd been in Luverne for four out of the last six weeks, I was feeling like one of the locals, and I told Fred that I'd stay with Dad for the first two weeks of hospice and then live with him at least three days a week after that. I suggested to Fred that he should get away from town every week, specifically when Tom and I were there. Fred said he'd think about it.

I was glad Fred expressed exactly where he stood and how far he could go, and I appreciated him for speaking his feelings. I knew Dad didn't realize how hard his living at home might be for me or Fred. He was now the child and we the parents. But it was hard to go against Dad's heartfelt wish to be at home.

Fred's long-standing, life-threatening illness had attuned him to the benefits of hospitalization. Doctors, other hospital personnel, and marvelous machines had saved or eased his life many times, and he had mentioned to me that during a crisis he felt safer and more relaxed within those white walls than outside them—particularly when he was able to develop a meaningful rapport with his doctors. Meanwhile, my view of hospitals was based on fewer contacts with hospital personnel and the underlying sense of being "frozen" or trapped, which I felt upon entering almost all institutions, a feeling I buried with half-fakey good cheer toward everyone I met. While Fred may have felt more powerful inside a hospital, I felt more helpless, maybe because in my life it had almost always been someone else who was ill, and as a bystander rather than a direct participant I truly had less say in what might happen from moment to moment. I could demand, suggest, beg, pray, or make wishes, but most decisions were made by the sick person or the hospital personnel, not by me.

I felt trapped between doing what was best for my gallant, chronically ill brother, who now had an ulcer to add to his troubles, and helping my father live and die as he wished. It was the hardest moment of Dad's illness for me, and as sometimes happens, only my anger and passion burned a clear view through my fear. Shaking, I told Fred that I was sorry about his ulcer, but I felt his statements about hospice might not turn out to be accurate. I said a hospice person would be at Dad's home at all times, possibly giving Fred and me more time to deal with the fact that our father was dying. I suggested that if Dad was happier at home, everyone might feel less stress. I pointed out (perhaps unfairly) that Fred hadn't stayed with Dad on the single night he did get home and hadn't seen how relaxed, joyful, and relieved Dad was or how he managed to talk about his impending death for the first (and the last) time. I added that I'd had several friends who got ulcers when their parents were dying, but their ulcers healed after their parents died. Fred's would heal, too (though I knew that Fred's body was always under considerably more stress because of his illness). But most important, I said, Dad had only a short time to live.

That night I spoke to Deb Vander Kooi, Ben's wife, who suggested a compromise: "How about taking your dad home only on weekends? But he'll have to be able to pivot and get into a wheelchair." I said that Dad couldn't do that, and she said he should work on his physical therapy until he could. I didn't tell Deb that I felt he'd be dead before physical therapy took effect, but I did tell her that if he came home for weekends, there would at least be a fifty-fifty chance he'd die at home, and I thanked her for the suggestion. Deb wished me good luck.

I called a friend, the playwright Marisha Chamberlain, and told her what was happening with my father. She said, "Your father needs the strongest kind of love and compassion right now, and you can give it to him. Don't worry about your brother now. Worry about your father."

Another friend and therapist, Olga Naud, advised, "You must trust your gut feelings about what to do with your father and for your father because your brother has made it clear that he has his own problems at this time. You are the only one left who does not have another agenda and who feels strong enough to be most empathetic to your father's needs. A dying person needs to be given the right to their dignity, especially a person like your dad, and if he wishes to go home, and it is at all possible to get him there, do so. Remember, even a few days a week will be a success for him!"

I longed to call Judith Grien, a writer from Luverne, who had said a month earlier that she admired Dad and his work and would be "delighted to stay with him as a hospice worker full time, with only four days off a month." But when I asked Dad about her, he said, "Oh, God, Freya, please don't call her. She's an extremely fine women, but I don't want a complex person who is a writer or wants to be a writer. I want a simple person who likes to sit in the sunshine and eat apples. Please!" So I dropped that idea and found other (part-time) help and told Dad that Tom and I would take him home the following weekend, whether the tube was out or not. Dr. Kuiper agreed that he would probably let us do that.

Dad stopped eating anything he didn't want. "Bread again," he would say, with great disgust, shoving it to the side of his plate. Chicken, which he'd never liked because it reminded him of cleaning chicken coops when he was a boy, really depressed him, but he would eat a small amount of beef or fish and cooked vegetables. He mostly wanted oatmeal and ice cream, preferably together, and we made sure he got it. Marya was bringing him fresh grapes and plums, which he enjoyed in very small helpings, and I asked Fred if he could cook some of Dad's beloved fresh fish in his apartment across the street and bring it over now and then. Tom and I bought boxes of sugarless ice cream bars and stored them behind the nurses' station.

Dad kept talking about the lovely woman in bed with him. Whoever she was, she made him happy. At other times he'd see his own half-bald head in the mirror across from him and say, "Who's that?"

"That's you."

"I don't think so," he said, looking terribly distressed.

"Well, who is it then, Dad?"

"Somebody visiting me," he said. "There are a lot of them now, all around me."

"There are people all around you?" I asked.

"Oh, yes, standing all around my bed. All the time. They want to talk with me."

"They're not bothering you?"

"No. They're fine people, every one of them, but they don't say much," he said.

And most touching, he kept saying, "Come on, now. We have to get moving. There's hay to be cut. Fields to be plowed. Come on."

"OK, Dad," I'd say.

"Where's Rowan? Where's Bly?"

"Right here, Dad."

"Well, tell them to hurry it up. We've got to get out to the fields and finish our work. Get after them, Freya, will you?"

"I will, Dad."

"I need them to help me finish the corn," he said.

He was back on the farm as a kid, helping his father harvest the corn and hay. Only now his grandchildren, Rowan and Bly, had become his helpmates, his dear younger brothers.

Christmas Day, December 1992
Dear Bly and Rowan,

I thought it would be nice if both of you grandsons received the same book from me.* I made it a point to read all the stories as well as the introductions to them. I'd read one story in one book and then the next story in the next book. Back and forth. So I've paged through both books.

Treasure these stories. Someday when you have your own families you can read the stories to your children: just as I once read *Alice through the Looking Glass* to your mother Freya; who in turn read Alice to you boys.

In the beginning you can skip the introductions. Later on, when you want to know more about where the stories came from, you can read them. Maybe someday you can write a theme for your English class about the introductions.

And maybe you won't like all the stories. Read only those that appeal to you, that you feel like they're "cool."

My Aunt Kathryn and my mother Alice read many of these stories to me when I was your age. We studied some of them in school. Besides these stories, Aunt Kathryn read me all of Hans Andersen's stories, the Mother Goose, and also from the Arabian Nights.

Merry Christmas. Life is good to me knowing I have such wonderful grandsons!

Love, Pake

The most wrenching time for me was Saturday of Labor Day weekend. Dad kept throwing back his sheets and trying to get out of bed, though he was too weak to move his legs. "Tell Tom to get the car, and I'm walking out of here!" he announced, like a general assembling his troops for one last campaign.

---

* This note accompanied two copies of *The Classic Fairy Tales*, published by Oxford University Press.

"Dad, Tom and I will take you home next weekend."

"C'mon, Freya, get Tom to pull my car up in front. We're going home now. Tom will carry me. He's a bull of a man."

"Dad, I'm sorry. We'll go soon. But we can't go home till the doctor releases you. Your lung is still draining."

"Well, I don't like to wait for things I want badly. Get Tom. We're going now. They keep waking me up here. In my house I can sleep."

I could not fully convince him that we'd take him home in a few days, that the doctors wanted him to stay. Tom finally told him (in the same words I had used, but to a greater effect) that Dr. Kuiper wanted him to wait a few more days. He stopped asking and said, "If I have to stay here, I will beg for a real pain pill because my tube hurts whenever I bump it."

As soon as the next nurse arrived, Tom and I asked for a "real" painkiller, but they gave him the usual: two Tylenol.

We brought up the matter of more serious pain relievers when Dr. Kuiper stopped by, but he said it would not help Dad to get too much more medication in him. So Dad said, smiling at Dr. Kuiper, "Oh, I'm just fine. Just give me two Tylenol, and I'll be fine."

He never wanted to go against what Dr. Kuiper said.

On Sunday of Labor Day weekend, Tom, Fred, and I watched the Vikings football game with Dad. Dad ate half a pan of apricot-raisin johnnycake Tom had baked for him, which he said reminded him of his childhood, and I brought him some sugarless ice cream to go with it. His roommate had been moved out because of a slight setback, and Dad was sitting up in a huge adjustable "Art Linkletter" lounge chair the nurses had dragged in from another part of the hospital. It had taken four nurses nearly an hour to move Dad from his bed into the chair, using a pulley, because he no longer had the strength to help them in any way. Straps were passed back and forth under his back and around his crotch, and two nurses pushed him into a sitting position while the others buckled and tied. Finally, they literally swung him, trussed up like a bale of hay, out of his bed and across the room and into his armchair. Dad protested mildly all the way, "I don't care for this. I like my bed. I can watch TV from my bed. I don't need this pulley. Tom can move me. I don't like this." Once he was established in the chair, however, he said he liked it and planned to stay there "forever, even to sleep at night." And he added, very firmly, "You nurses can just move my bed out and give it to someone who needs it. I'll be sleeping in this chair."

> Let's start a cult in which we make heroes out of such ornery cusses as we may still have around—out of our lone wolves, go-it-a-loners, dissenters, hermits, screwballs, aginers. Such a fad, the fad of the ornery cuss or the odd ball, might save us. It is still a truth that the health of a society can be measured by the size and the vigor of its minority group.
>
> In fact, I'd like to recommend that every village and town go out of its way to make sure it still has an ornery cuss in its midst. At least one. And should any village discover it doesn't have an honorable dissenter around, I'd like to suggest that the mayor declare a state of emergency until such a citizen can be found.
> "Wanted: More Ornery Cusses"
> *Prime Fathers*

Later the nurses had to move Dad back into his bed because he couldn't sit up in the chair for more than an hour. This time Tom and Fred helped them, and they didn't use the pulley.

"How are you going to move him once he gets home?" Fred asked me out in the hall.

"I won't. I'll just prop him up with pillows or turn him to one side or the other," I said.

"He'll get bedsores if he isn't moved."

"I don't think he'll be around long enough to worry about bedsores. Dr. Kuiper says we can take him home in three days if the drainage tube is removed."

"What if the tube can't be removed?"

"Dr. Kuiper says Dad can go home even with the tube for two days, just to get a break from the hospital."

The next morning we decided to take Rowan and Bly back to Minneapolis to start eighth grade. They wanted to be there for the first three days, partly because there was a special two-day camping trip for student-and-teacher "bonding," and they wanted to join their friends.

When I explained to Dad that we'd drive back in three days to take him home to Roundwind, he looked a little surprised, as he always did when I said I was leaving. I had told him several times the night before that we would be gone briefly, but he didn't have the same sense of time—some days passed like weeks, others like minutes, and he spent much of the day sleeping.

I stroked Dad's cheek and said good-bye, and he looked at me and mumbled a few semigarbled words. I understood that he was reciting or quoting from something he'd read, but I had to bend close to hear him. He said basically, "Yes. Good-bye, Dolly. Your path leads upward into life, and my path leads downward to death." He shook his head in wonder. "Isn't that a wonderful saying? A genius wrote that. It's so beautiful. What a wonderful writer. Just wonderful."

He then spoke the name of the person who had written those words, but I could not understand him. (Art Huseboe says it sounds like the original source of such quotations, Socrates in Plato's "The Apology": "The hour of departure has arrived, and we go our ways—I to die, and you to live. Which is better only God knows.") I didn't want to ask him to repeat himself because he looked so tired and pained when people didn't understand him. Also it was the first time he had mentioned dying to me since he went home for just one day on August 17.

I believe one part of Dad knew he was about to die, and another part of him did not accept it. The father in him, the man in him, and the farmer in him knew it and acknowledged it. The other being inside him, the creative being, the lizard prince and dedicated novelist, did not accept, would not accept, and should not have accepted his death.

We got home in the late afternoon on Labor Day, and I snorkeled in the lake. I felt privileged to swim freely and dreamily through the silver-green underwater plants and the blue-green swarming fish, but I kept thinking of my father trapped in his hospital bed.

The next morning I woke feeling cold all over my body, even though it was very hot outside. I stayed in bed to keep warm, talking on the phone, making arrangements for oxygen tanks for Dad's weekend trips home, and looking for more nursing help. That evening I called Fred to see how Dad was doing, but he wasn't in, so I left a message on his answering machine.

Around 9:00 P.M. Art Huseboe called and said he was worried. He'd driven over from Sioux Falls to visit with Dad, but no one could rouse him. One nurse said to Art, "It has not been a good day. Mr. Manfred might be lapsing into a coma. I wonder if I should call the family?" Art hung up on a positive note, saying that Dad would probably fool everybody and "rise up again" as he always had over the past six weeks.

I called the nurse on duty. She verified that Dad had been impossible to rouse all day but said he'd had a "good spell" at

9:30, after Art left. "He ate ice cream and oatmeal and talked appropriately." I called Fred back to tell him what Art and the nurse had said. Fred went across the street to check on Dad and called me back to tell me that Dad had normal blood pressure, a normal heartbeat, and normal kidney function, but he hadn't been able to take medications and had only spoken for a few minutes that morning and again at 9:30 that evening. Fred said he'd call me Wednesday morning to tell me if Dad was slipping into a coma because I wanted to see Dad again before that happened.

When Fred hung up, I told Tom that Dad was not going to make it until the weekend; he was dying, and I wanted to drive down that night. Tom said it wasn't wise to drive from midnight until 4:00 A.M. when we were both so tired. "Let's wait until Fred calls us tomorrow," he said. And I agreed. I lay awake all night, feeling I should jump into the car and start driving.

On Wednesday morning I sat by the phone. When Fred had not called me by noon, I called him. He said he was just going to call. "Dad ate cereal and milk for breakfast. His drainage tube is still in and still discharging pus and blood. When I asked him a question, he took one breath in but gave no answer. Dr. Kuiper says he's taken another slip." Fred added that he and Marya had just had lunch with Dad and that he spoke briefly, but it was garbled. The nurses indicated that he was slipping toward a coma.

I said, "We're on our way."

As I was speaking Marya banged on Fred's door, hollering, "Fred, they want you at the hospital right now." Fred said, "I'd better go." He hung up.

Ten minutes later the phone rang, and Fred said, "Freya, is Tom there?"

I knew when I heard his question that Dad was dead. "He's dead, isn't he?"

"Yes, he died a few minutes ago. Just when the one o'clock whistle for the emergency warning system blew here in town. The nurse was holding his hand and he died."

Tom, working downstairs, heard me groan. He came running up from his office. Fred said the hospital would hold Dad's body until we got there.

> Horse, I give you to Wakantanka. I shall let you lie upon the rocks. I do this that the elements may take you back: the spirits your white coat, the air your lungs, the earth your blood, the rocks your bones, the worms your flesh. It was from all these that you were formed and it is to all these that you must return. Life is a circle. The power of the world works always in circles. All things try to be round. Life is all one. It begins in one place, it flows for a time, it returns to one place. The earth is all that lasts. I have said. Yelo.
> *Conquering Horse*

Months later Dr. Kuiper told me he had a "vivid memory" of Marya and Fred coming out the back door of their apartment building toward the hospital. He said Dad had eaten a good lunch and was "talking and appropriate" that morning when he'd stopped by. But thirty minutes after lunch, when a nurse went to check on him, he was in "agonal respiration," which is breathing with twenty- to thirty-second pauses between each breath. It's "like sleeping and forgetting to breathe; there was no struggle and it was real peaceful." Dr. Kuiper said he was talking on the phone with Dr. Shaw at Mayo about whether to finish Dad's radiation treatments when a nurse said Mr. Manfred was "having difficulty breathing." He cut the call short and was at Dad's side "within three minutes," but Dad was gone.

I asked how the physical part of dying worked, and Dr. Kuiper said, "The lungs stop first and can't pump, and then the heart goes into arrhythmia and can't pump, and then you have a multisystem shutdown. It happens very peacefully and completely—it's so fast." Then he added, "But I feel it's OK, as I had visions of your dad lingering for months. In many ways he did it his way." He added that Dad's death "surprised us, though the nurses were not as surprised because they remembered that when they'd rolled him over to wash him that morning his back was mottled." Mottling usually means the heart is not sending blood to the extremities but trying instead to keep the body alive by directing blood to the heart, kidneys, liver, and other vital organs. "But when I saw your dad that morning I was not informed about the mottling, and the nurses later realized they should have mentioned this to me." If they had, Fred might have called me, and I might have been with Dad when he died.

Dr. Kuiper recorded the cause of death as "Central Nervous System Lymphoma" because this is what ultimately led to Dad's other problems. Contributing factors were sepsis and pneumonia. "Fifty percent of the people who get gram negative sepsis in the bloodstream do not survive," he said, "but your dad survived the sepsis. Unfortunately, that battle, along with his other battles, exhausted him." I asked what had caused Dad's occasional disorientation during the last three weeks of his life since the brain cancer had been "considerably reduced" after two and a half weeks of radiation. Dr. Kuiper said that Dad's confusion was probably caused by the stress of various complications and never by the brain tumor or brain swelling. He added that this was "a very difficult family to forget and a very difficult process for me as a doctor because I was so fond of Frederick, and so wanted to help him continue to be a writer." He said Dad was "amazing and special and always himself and wonderful. The last time you left, Freya, we all thought he'd be around a few more weeks, and we were going to help you try to get him home at least for two days at a time before he died." I said that Dad had mentioned "the road to death" when I left him forty-eight hours before, and Dr. Kuiper said, "Yes, patients usually know when they are dying."

Karen Roberts and Eileen Hocking were the two Luverne nurses who were with Dad when he died. Karen said, "When I came that morning his breathing and coloring were not good, and he didn't talk much. He was semiconscious. At eleven-thirty lunch he would open his mouth for oatmeal and ice cream if we held the spoon to his mouth, but he didn't speak, except when I asked him if he had any pain. Then he said, very clearly, 'No.' He said nothing more. About forty minutes after lunch, we noticed a difference in his breathing, and Eileen and I stood by him, and I held his hand. I don't know if he knew I was holding his hand. I never know if patients know these things, but I like to think they do. There was no struggle. He went peacefully like he was ready, like all of a sudden he made the decision."

> Reverend Creed's voice became solemn. "He was a true hero. He fought to save his own life, yes. He fought to save the lives of his boys, yes. He fought to save all our lives in Bighorn County, yes. But he did more than that. He fought not knowing his side would win. That is his true glory. He fought because he was a man and because bravery was expected of him. He fought because he had lived by a code and because he wanted to die by that code. Though his heart might be in mortal anguish, though the terror of death might be in his throat, he fought anyway, calmly and well. He shed his blood that men might once again learn that you cannot force a free people to accept something they do not want.
> *Riders of Judgment*

Tom and I picked up the boys at school. They were sitting out on the grass in front of the building, weeping. We got out of the car to hug them, and a few of their friends called out the windows, "Sorry about your Grandpa!" Then we made the long drive to Luverne.

"Should I go in and see Pake?" Rowan asked as we drove.

"If you want to," I said. "Whatever you feel like doing is best."

"Are you going to look at him?"

"Yes. I want to, even though his spirit or life force is gone, and I'll only see his body."

"Why?" Bly asked. "Why will you go in?"

"Because he's my father. I love him even when he's dead."

"But if he's dead he's not really there in a way," Bly said.

"It's a little scary," Tom said.

"Yeah," Bly said.

"I'll go in," Rowan said. "Bly won't. He's too scared."

"Am not! I'll decide when I get there," Bly said.

"Good idea," Tom said.

> *December 29, 1986*
> *Dear Freya and Tom and boys,*
>
> The boys are sweethearts. It's good to see they are growing up quite strong-minded and at the same time considerate. That's the whole secret of a good upbringing—that one grows up with a strong ego that other people love. It takes quite some expert sailing between all sorts of dangerous shoals to get a child into manhood or womanhood safely.
>
> You're both doing a helluva job.
> *Dad.*

When we drove up to the hospital, Tom and I told Rowan and Bly that they didn't have to come inside with us but that we wanted to see Dad. They said they'd think about it. They got out of the car and watched us go in.

As I approached Dad's room, a nurse stopped me, but when I explained I wanted to see my father, she said to go in. I went in and had a moment alone with him. All his tubes and other paraphernalia were gone. He still had half of his hair, having lost much of it as a result of the radiation, and his hawk nose rose above his long face. He looked more like Uncle Ed, whom I'd seen in his coffin in February, than he ever had because his brilliant eyes were closed, and his ruddy coloring was gone. His huge long hands lay over his chest. I drew closer, and it seemed to me that at any moment he would take a breath. Might even get mad at me for waking him. It seemed as if it would be such a small thing for him to move one hand or one finger, but it was the biggest thing in the world and he didn't.

Rowan came in, sad and wondering, and stood next to Pake and began to cry. Bly entered the room more slowly, his open fourteen-year-old face afraid, curious, sad. The nurse was there, too, hovering. Finally I told her we wanted to be alone with Dad, and although she hesitated for some reason, she did leave. "Get out! Get out!" my heart was shouting. "Let us be alone!"

We had a moment or two as a family, and I touched Dad's right hand, so cold, and then the crook of his right elbow, still warm. We were crying. Tom started to talk to the boys the way he and I like to talk to them at important times, sharing what is happening, asking them how they are feeling.

Then Fred, and finally, Marya, came in, though I was suddenly desperate to be alone with Dad. I assumed they'd already been with him as he'd been lying there for six hours or more.

Later I had more time to be alone with Dad while Tom talked with Fred, and Rowan and Bly went outside. I sat next to Dad and touched his arm. I didn't want to leave him, and I imagined sitting near him for a few days or having him come home with us in the car, dead as he was, just so I could be near his body. I wondered why we put people in boxes, in graves. Why not set them out where sun and rain can dissolve them?

> "Let the white man hide his dead in the ground if he is ashamed of them. That is his way. But the red man keeps his dead in sight so that he may remember them. That is his way." The scarlet plume at the back of his head twiggled a little in the soft breeze. "Later when the flesh has departed, and there is nothing left but the bones, then the red man returns the bones to the earth his mother."
>
> *Scarlet Plume*

I uncovered and looked at Dad's broad chest, his incredibly long and beautiful white legs and bony knees, and the long feet, tortured by bunions. I looked around the gray room and saw that the window was closed again. I opened it and let in the smell of street dust, mowed grass, and flowers. The soft loose pink roses outside his window had dropped some of their sweet September petals on the gravel. Fall was coming.

I tucked Dad in, broke off some goldenrod from the bouquet I'd picked for him on Labor Day, and placed the sprig in his right hand. I took the rest of the wildflowers from the vase, got in the car with Tom and the boys, and dropped the flowers, one at a time, on the road between the hospital and Roundwind. I wanted Dad's spirit to be able to find the path from the hospital where he'd suffered and endured to the home where he wanted to live and die. I kept four flowers: when we got to Roundwind, Rowan took one and dropped it north of the house, facing Blue Mound; Bly took another and dropped it on the east side, where the sun rises; Tom walked south of the house and dropped a flower by the long driveway; and I walked west, into the setting sun, and dropped a flower there.

The next morning I woke at 5:00 and went out into the wet grass for a walk. When I was about ten feet from the front door, a piercing cry greeted me. "Akkkk!" Startled, I looked up and saw a hawk hovering straight above me, a big hawk. As I stood staring, the hawk cried, "Akkkk!" again, dipped its wings toward the earth for an instant, and then flew toward the rising sun.

I knew the hawk at once.

I felt the hawk was my father's spirit, which had followed our path of flowers from the hospital and spent the night with us at Roundwind one last time.

In all my early morning walks at Roundwind, no other hawk had ever greeted me, or, once sighted, flown on so steadily, so surely, or so far, as if its final destination were some tree in Siouxland, or the sun.

"Father Hawk," I whispered. "Father Hawk, farewell."

"Patience and brilliance is all."
March 30, 1994
(Frederick Manfred's last journal entry)

EPILOGUE

THREE DREAMS

THE WORST OF MY GRIEF AFTER DAD DIED WAS THAT I could no longer see him or touch him. His thoughts and feelings were in his books, his letters, his essays, and his poems. But his face, his huge hands, his wide, thick shoulders—all of these were gone. I longed for one physical remnant of him that couldn't be taken from me. A writer friend told me that only when he was able to dream of his dead mother did he finally accept her death. Another writer friend told me you don't dream of someone who has died until you have fully accepted that they are, in fact, dead. Both of these remarks felt meaningless to me, something that sounded true for my friends, but not based on my own truth. The absence of my father's presence sometimes hit me so hard that I would fall face down on the floor and weep without tears. I didn't believe I could accept Dad's death even if I did dream about him. "Life," as Carl Jung said, "can never believe in death."

Over time I settled on the hope that he would return to me in my dreams. But no dream came after his funeral or after the memorial at Roundwind a month later. I waited, counting the days, the weeks, the months. Each night before I fell asleep I asked my dreams to bring news of him. My dreams didn't answer though they'd never failed me before.

Finally, six months after he died, I had my first dream

about Dad. He was lying on his old porch swing reading a thick book. As I approached him, he put one forefinger between the pages to hold his place and smiled, happy to see me. He was wearing the old green-and-black checked shirt that he used to call his "lumberjack shirt, like the one Paul Bunyan wore." In life he had often worn it when he chopped wood, and when I'd asked him if I could wear it for art classes my freshman year at Macalester College, he'd handed it to me without a word. I also wore the shirt outside of art class, even when some of my friends teased me about how ridiculously large and unfashionable it was. I wore it, I now realize, because it made me feel less lonely.

At any rate, I was very glad to see my father again. I sat beside him on the edge of the swing and gently stroked the wooly arm of the shirt. After a while he said, "It's going to be all right, Dolly. It's going to be all right." He repeated this phrase quietly, over and over, as we rocked to and fro. At some point I began to wonder if he meant that things were going to be all right for him, or for me. When I looked more closely at him to find out, his smile said he hoped it would be me.

A year went by without another dream about my father. I often thought of that first dream, and it comforted me to know I had been able to "visit" with him at least once and that some part of me felt things *were* going to be "all right" without him. I wanted whatever small certainty I could muster in the face of death. I wanted to live centered, without falling apart, giving up, or losing my place in the world.

After months of thinking about the wonderful things I missed about my father, I found myself meditating on the most difficult aspect of his relationship with me. This was the feeling that sometimes, around him, I didn't exist. Or rather, I did exist, not as a human being, but as a tree. Every now and then I felt, palpably, as if I had roots, a trunk, limbs, and leaves; Dad talked so much and at such length with such glee and charm and abandon that there was no time or need for me to speak. I existed only as his tree friend, solid and silent, waving my branches in the breeze of his speech.

At times becoming a friendly mute tree enraged me. I needed to talk, too. At other times I enjoyed being a tree. And even when I felt enraged with Dad, I also always felt stronger simply because he existed. He was honest, positive, and grateful to be alive but also welling with thankfulness that I existed, that Tom existed, that Rowan and Bly existed. He was a safe companion. He did not invade my boundaries or refuse to see my point of view or accuse me of being idiotic if I reacted strongly to whatever he said.

My father's next dream visit occurred on his birthday, January 6, a year and four months after his death.

I was sleeping alone in our king-size bed because Tom had the flu and had moved down to sleep in his studio. A tall figure draped in a long black shroud or monk's habit entered my room. The figure stopped and stood at the end of the bed in the full moonlight. I sat bolt upright and saw it was my father. He never came closer, though I wanted him to, and he spoke firmly, with tears standing out on his cheeks like white opals.

"I'm sorry I never knew you, dear," he said. "I'm sorry I never *really* knew you."

He repeated these words over and over, his face full of self-recognition. He had watched me grow up, "knowing" me with his sentient artist's ability to see the human heart and soul, yet in some other basic way he had not known me. He'd shared thoughts and feelings many fathers do not dream of sharing with their daughters and heard thoughts and feelings many fathers will never hear from their daughters, but he'd also missed something else worth knowing.

But the chance was gone. In this dream he and I were not angry. We were accepting our relationship.

I find the end of the dream rather wonderful. After he said for perhaps the tenth time, "I'm sorry I never really knew you, dear," I asked him (with my eyes) to stop talking.

He became silent and looked at me, and I said, "That's OK, Dad. Because I knew *you*. Because I knew *you*."

The giant black form of my father stared at me. His eyes met mine with full understanding and love. For that one moment he mirrored back to me that my love for him had been a great love. It required no absolute return.

And then I awoke and he was gone.

A great deal was salvaged in this dream. My father gave me love and truth. If he came again, in any dream, I would answer truly and lovingly back to him.

In the nearly four years after my father's death, Tom and I experienced a litany of physical and financial disasters. Uncle Henry, my father's youngest and favorite brother, died of cancer in May 1996, a year and eight months after my father. How we miss him. Other wonderful friends and acquaintances died, too.

Also during this period my husband's free-lance screenwriting jobs began to dwindle at just the point when his understanding of the art of screenwriting and his abilities as a screenwriter were at their peak. (Random House did, however, publish his witty and profound book about screenwriting, *Good Scripts, Bad Scripts*.) I experienced a similar dearth of publication and was unable to place some of the best poetry I'd ever written or any of my novels or children's stories—ten years' worth of writing. This pattern was all the more frustrating because ninety percent of my rejections had one theme, "We loved this moving book, but we can't publish it because our marketing people tell us we won't sell enough copies in the present publishing atmosphere."

I also regret that my father never saw our new home, which I love, and which we may have to sell. I've written some of my best poems in our boathouse beside Christmas Lake, a place to which I am irretrievably attached. I've transplanted my father's blue iris and orange tiger lilies from his yard at Roundwind to our garden. My father's mother's favorite herb for tea, purple bergamot, dug from the prairie near Luverne, sprouts beside our sunny deck. Not to mention every type of lilac Tom and I could dig up from our first home in Bloomington, the same lilacs Dad brought down to Luverne when he left Bloomington in 1959.

Most disturbing, our twin teenage sons became very ill for more than two months and then for several long years began slowly recovering from a "mono-like" illness they contracted in the winter of their freshman year of high school. Although an internal specialist says the "mono-like" thing is gone, their postviral fatigue syndrome—from which they have finally recovered—changed all of our lives emotionally, physically, and spiritually.

With all of this and more hanging over my head, on Memorial Day, in the morning hours of Monday, May 26, 1997, I had this dream:

Tom and I and the kids were living temporarily in another city with which we were only slightly familiar. The kids had to attend school; Tom and I had to work.

Tom and I awoke at 6 A.M. and decided to run errands in our battered maroon Pontiac. We planned to return home in time to wake the kids for school and feed them breakfast. We set out through the winding, unfamiliar streets of our new city, disagreeing on the day's schedule.

"Let's get some food from the store and make a big family breakfast," I said.

"Sorry, Freya, I'll shop for food with you, but I want to work."

"But I want to spend more time with you. So do the kids. I feel lonely and off base in this strange city."

"So do I. But I'll see you all for dinner tonight."

"Tom, I can't tell you how much it would mean to me if we could all have breakfast together."

"No. I'm worried that I won't finish my work."

As we pulled up at the store, Tom announced that he'd save even more time by getting gas for the car while I shopped for food alone.

"Oh, great, now I'm doing the shopping alone! I thought you wanted to come in!"

"I do, but it's late. I'll be back in a few minutes and drive you home with the groceries."

Tom drove off, leaving me at the store.

Moments later, when I stepped out of the store with my purchases I couldn't see Tom anywhere. I walked up and down in front of the store, recognizing a few buildings but totally unfamiliar with most of them. I didn't leave the block because I was hoping to spot our car and wave to Tom so we could hurry home and he could get to work.

Time passed. I began to imagine how annoyed Tom must be, looking for me, not finding me, wanting to get to work. Then I began to picture how the kids would feel waking up without us. They'd be ok because they had each other, but they'd be worried, too.

I decided Tom must have lost his way so I circled the block, returned to the store, and then circled another block. My eyes searched the alien streets. Once I saw our car, making the turn at a far corner, and I waved desperately, but Tom was looking just as desperately the other way and did not see me amid the heavy traffic and winding streets. Sometimes I ran, sometimes I walked, carrying the heavy groceries, always circling within a few blocks of the store but always missing Tom.

I began to despair. I'd have to forget about Tom and take a taxi back to the kids, who were certainly awake by now. I wasn't even sure how to tell the cab driver to get to our apartment. I didn't know the roads and couldn't recall the façade of our new apartment building.

Suddenly a car pulled up next to me, driven by a cheerful woman with a four-year-old girl and a two-year-old boy beside her in the front seat. The back door of the car opened, and there sat my father, smiling out at me.

"Freya!" he cried. "Come on in! You need a lift?"

It was all the more surprising to see him because I knew, of course, that my father was dead. He'd been dead for almost three years.

"Dad! How are you!"

"Good!" he said.

His big face was red with pleasure at seeing me and—equally important to both of us—at being able to give me a lift. He was wearing blue work pants and a blue work shirt. I hopped into the back seat with him, and he gave me a warm hug.

"Don't worry," he said. "We'll drive you back to your place." The woman in front drove on, knowing exactly where she was going through the winding streets, the two kids beside her staring curiously back at me.

"You and Tom had trouble connecting?" he asked.

"Yes. He's probably very upset. Probably still driving around somewhere."

"He'll find his way home eventually," Dad said, "and you'll be there."

As we drove along, I kept looking for Tom's car, thinking

of him and our sons, but suddenly I realized, my God, my father is dead and he's come back to help me, and I'm not even asking him any questions.

"Dad, by the way—how is it for you?"

"How is it?"

"Where you are now—how is it?"

"Oh, it's fine."

"But—is it hard to be where you are?"

"No, it's great. I'm very busy and involved the whole day long."

"And who . . . ?"

"Oh, these people here? The woman and kids are with me. She loves to drive the car, so I let her. And this little boy is hers. He's real smart, strong as an ox. And this little sweetie is hers, too. She's a real pal. She doesn't miss a trick. She's subtle. And brilliant. And sometimes she's a little dickens, too."

"And . . . and they're dead, like you?"

He laughed. "What do you mean, 'dead,' Freya? I'm alive. Very much alive!"

I could see, then, that he was. The perception that he was a dead man driving around the city with two dead children and a dead woman vanished instantly in the face of a new reality: he was alive because he said he was.

"We're near your place now," he said. And, with a flourish, he added, "I'll escort you in, like a gentleman."

He got out of the car and walked arm in arm with me into the building and up to our floor, where I found Tom sitting on the bed and the kids awake. I raced over to Tom.

"I'm back! I'm so glad to see you! And guess what, you'll never guess what!!"

"What?" Tom said.

"My dad brought me home!"

"Your dad?"

"Yes. He's alive! And he gave me a ride home."

"Alive?" Tom said, wonder in his face.

I turned and beckoned with great excitement for Dad to come forward. He lingered in the shadows, looking at me as if he were ready to leave. He shook his head, still smiling happily because he'd been able to give me a lift. "I'm going," he said. "Now you're home with Tom."

"Don't go! Say hi to Tom for a minute!"

"No, I have to go now. You'll be fine," he said.

Tom got up to see Dad, but before he could pop his head around the corner into the hallway where Dad was standing, my father faded into the shadows, the blue of his work clothes blending into the dark stairwell.

When I woke up, I thought of the many gifts my father had given me, both in life and in death. What had been his most valued gift to me? How did I remember him?

Simply put, my father gave me "a lift," a gift he delighted in giving more times than I can count. He helped others, too—I saw him stop, smiling and confident and proud, to help his students, friends, and family. When I was young, he didn't mind sadness or being lost. He often cried himself and said that feeling lost was rather a good thing. But he didn't feel comfortable if any of us was angry or afraid. "Best keep anger to yourself," he'd say. Or, "No need to talk about being afraid—I'm here with you now so you'll be fine." As I got older, my father stopped taking my anger or fear so personally; he concentrated less on his reactions to my emotions and more on what I was feeling. If I said I was angry or afraid, he'd say, "You're passionate. Just like Uncle Herm. Or Uncle Hank. But they did just fine. And, besides, I'm here now!" And we'd laugh, knowing that his being there was both the most and the least important part of what was happening.

My father had a way of *being there* as a positive, life-affirming force. It wasn't just that he helped me because he loved me; he got such joy out of his power to help. He loved knowing that I would be safe because he was safe and because I had let him lend a hand. The question of whether he always felt so positive about life didn't arise—he made up his mind to be a man who gave people a lift.

I'm thankful for this third dream of Dad. Thankful for its arrival on Memorial Day during difficult times. I'll be telling our sons this dream at dinner tonight. They'll squirm and say, "Can we go now?" but secretly they'll be honored and pleased that I shared this dream.

This dream meets my need for ancestral attachments, a need to return to ceremonious standards of love and remembrance, and a need to believe that we are not alone, that we bear a mutual responsibility for each other. If you're lost, separated from the ones you love, alone in a strange city, it will be my pleasure to give you a lift, with the understanding that in the end I'll leave you at your work, to live your own life, and continue with mine.

My father came by to give me a lift because, as he says, he's very much alive—and if *he* says he's alive, he is: busy working all day long. He came to me in what we call "dreams," but they are more than dreams. They are real moments that can't last forever but that sustain life and give everlasting strength.

May Dad give me a lift again, when I need it.

ACKNOWLEDGMENTS

Thanks to everyone who wished Frederick Manfred well, especially those who told me stories about him. I welcome more!

Thanks to Carol Bly for her profound understanding of what I was trying to do in my first, short version of this memoir. Her clear, honest comments encouraged me to continue.

Thanks to Bill Holm for his bighearted, brotherly response and for inviting me to read portions of the early manuscript in his classroom.

Thanks to Philip Roth, Robert Bly, and Ruth Bly for their comments on the finished manuscript, their wholeness of perception, and their enlightened passion.

Thanks to Wendy Schmalz of Harold Ober & Associates, an enthusiastic agent and champion of this book.

Thanks to Ann Regan and Sally Rubinstein at the Minnesota Historical Society Press and to my copy editor, Mary Byers, who cared for this book as I always hoped people in charge of publishing and editing might.

Thanks to my brother, Fred, sister, Marya, and mother, Maryanna, for embracing this book as one version of the larger truth.

And thanks most of all to my sons, Rowan and Bly Pope, who loved their Pake and sustain me in his absence, and my husband, Tom Pope, who helped me before, during, and after the writing of this book and whose presence is a marvel only the ghost of Frederick Manfred could conceivably grasp.

At Christmas Lake, Minnesota, 1999

Frederick Manfred: A Daughter Remembers was designed and set in type by Will Powers at the Minnesota Historical Society Press. The typeface is Miller Text, an interpretation by Matthew Carter of the classic Scotch typefaces of the early nineteenth century. This book was printed and bound by Bang Printing, Brainerd, Minnesota.